iCONLOGiC ™
"Skills and Drills" Learning

Version: v051623
Page Count: 202
9781960604002 (Print Book)
97819606040021 (VitalSource PDF)
9781960604019 (eBook)

TechSmith Camtasia 2023:
The Essentials

"Skills and Drills" Learning

Kevin Siegel

iCONLOGiC
"Skills and Drills" Learning

Contents

NOTES

NOTES

iCONLOGiC

"Skills and Drills" Learning

About This Book

This Section Contains Information About:

NOTES

The Author

Kevin Siegel is a Certified Technical Trainer (CTT), Certified Master Trainer (CMT), and Certified Online Training Professional (COTP). Kevin served in the U.S. Coast Guard, where he was twice decorated with the Coast Guard's Achievement Medal. He also received the coveted Alex Haley Award for writing and photojournalism.

Kevin has spent decades as a technical communicator, face-to-face and virtual trainer, eLearning developer, publisher, and keynote speaker. Kevin has written hundreds of books for adult learners. Some of his best-selling titles include "Adobe Captivate: The Essentials," "Articulate Storyline: The Essentials," and "TechSmith Camtasia: The Essentials."

IconLogic

Founded by Kevin in 1992, IconLogic is a training, development, and publishing company offering services to clients across the globe.

As a **training** company, IconLogic has directly trained tens of thousands of professionals both on-site and online on a variety of applications. Our training clients include some of the largest companies in the world such as Adobe Systems, Inc., Urogen Pharma, Agilent Technologies, Sanofi Pasteur, Kelsey-Seybold Clinic, FAA, Office Pro, Adventist Health Systems, AGA, AAA, Wells Fargo, VA.gov, American Express, Lockheed Martin, General Mills, Grange Insurance, General Dynamics Electric Boat, Michigan.gov, Freddie Mac, Fannie Mae, ADP, ADT, Federal Reserve Bank of Richmond, Walmart, Kroger, Duke Energy, USCG, USMC, Canadian Blood, PSA, Department of Homeland Security, and the Department of Defense.

As a **development** company, IconLogic has produced eLearning and technical documentation for Duke Energy, World Bank, Heineken, EVERFI, Bank of America, Fresenius Kabi, Wells Fargo, Federal Express, Fannie Mae, American Express, Microsoft, Department of For-Hire Vehicles, DC Child and Family Services Agency, DCORM, Canadian Blood Services, Cancer.org, MLB, Archrock, NEEF, CHUBB Limited, Canadian Natural Resources, and Hagerty Insurance.

As a **publishing** company, IconLogic has published hundreds of critically acclaimed books and created technical documents for both print and digital publication. Some of our most popular titles over the years include books on HTML, Virtual Reality, Dreamweaver, QuarkXPress, PageMaker, InDesign, Word, Excel, Access, Publisher, RoboHelp, RoboDemo, iSpring Suite, Presenter, Storyline, Captivate, Camtasia, and PowerPoint.

You can learn more about IconLogic's varied services at www.iconlogic.com.

Book Conventions

In our experience, people learn best by doing, not just by watching or listening. With this concept in mind, instructors and authors with years of experience training adult learners have created IconLogic books. IconLogic books typically contain a minimal amount of text and are loaded with hands-on activities, screen captures, and confidence checks to reinforce newly acquired skills. This book is divided into modules. Because each module builds on lessons taught in a previous module, it is recommended that you complete each module in succession.

Lesson Key

Instructions for you to follow look like this:

❑ choose **File > Open**

If you are expected to type anything or if something is important, it is set in bold type like this:

❑ type **9** into the text field

If you are expected to press a key on your keyboard, the instruction looks like this:

❑ press [**shift**]

Confidence Checks

As you work through this book, you will come across the Confidence Check image at the right. Throughout each module, you are guided through hands-on, step-by-step activities. To help ensure that you are grasping the content, Confidence Checks encourage you to complete a process or steps on your own—without step-by-step guidance. Because some of the book's activities build on completed Confidence Checks, you should complete each of the activities and Confidence Checks in order.

Software & Asset Requirements

To complete the lessons presented in this book, you will need TechSmith Camtasia version 2023 installed on your computer. Camtasia does not come with this book, but a free trial version can be downloaded from TechSmith.com.

You will need to download some free Camtasia projects and media assets that have been created specifically to support this book and this version of Camtasia (see the "Camtasia 2023 Project Assets" section below).

Because you will be importing, recording, and editing audio, ensure that you have a headset or a computer with speakers and a microphone.

You will learn how to incorporate Microsoft PowerPoint presentations into Camtasia projects. To complete those activities, you will need PowerPoint installed on your computer.

NOTES

Camtasia 2023 Project Assets

To help you get started with learning Camtasia, I have provided you with all of the Camtasia projects and media assets you need to get started except the Camtasia 2023 software. I call these assets data files, and they include several projects, videos, images, audio files, and more. The step-by-step instructions for downloading the data files from my website are shown below.

As you work through this book, pretend that you work for Super Simplistic Solutions, a fictional company in Anytown, USA. As the lead corporate trainer and professional eLearning developer, your job is to create all of the corporate training videos using TechSmith Camtasia.

Download and Extract the Data Files

1. Download the support files that accompany this book.

   ☐ start a web browser and go to the following website: **iconlogic.com/data**

   ☐ depending on your platform, click either **PC** or **Mac**

   ☐ from the **TechSmith Camtasia Data Files** area, click the **Camtasia 2023: The Essentials** link

   Techsmith Camtasia Data Files ⌃

   - Camtasia 2023: The Essentials
   - Camtasia 2022: The Essentia Camtasia 2023 The Essentials Data Files
   - Camtasia 2021: The Essentials

   The download is a zipped file containing several folders and files.

2. Once you have successfully downloaded the assets to your computer, locate and extract the contents of the file. Depending upon which version you downloaded, the file name is either **Camtasia2023Data_PC or Camtasia2023Data_Mac**.

   Once unzipped, there should be a folder on your computer named **Camtasia2023Data_PC** or **Mac**. Shown below is the **Camtasia2022Data_PC folder**. While the folder structure is identical between the Mac and PC, the Camtasia project files contained are specific to the Mac or PC operating systems.

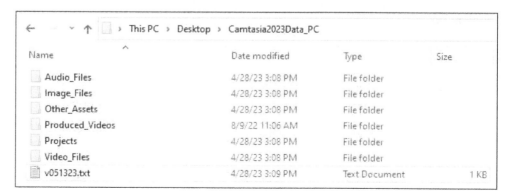

How TechSmith Software Updates Affect This Book

This book was written specifically to teach you how to use TechSmith Camtasia **version 2023**. At the time this book was written (May 2023), Camtasia 2023 was the latest and greatest version of Camtasia available from TechSmith.

The specific version of the Camtasia **2023** software used for the screenshots shown throughout this book is **2023.0.2**. You can check your Camtasia version by choosing **Help > About Camtasia** if you're on a PC; if you're on a Mac, choose **Camtasia 2023 > About Camtasia**.

With each major release of Camtasia, my intention is to publish a book to support that version and make it available within 30-60 days of the software being released by TechSmith. Between major annual updates, TechSmith tends to update Camtasia frequently to fix bugs or add functionality. An updated version might be called Camtasia **2023.0.3** or perhaps **2023.1.x**.

The software updates from TechSmith are usually bug fixes and have little to no impact on the lessons presented in my books. However, TechSmith might make a significant change to the way Camtasia looks or behaves, even with a minor update. For instance, when TechSmith updated Camtasia from version 8.3 to 8.4, several features were changed which caused confusion for readers of that book.

Because it is not possible for me to recall nor update printed books, some instructions you are asked to follow in this book may not match your patched/updated version of Camtasia. If something on your screen does not match what is shown in the book, visit our Errata page on the IconLogic website or contact me directly at **ksiegel@iconlogic.com**. Use your smartphone's camera on the image at the right to be taken directly to our Errata page.

If you are using a more recent version of Camtasia than was used to create the projects for this book, you may see a dialog box asking if you would like to update the project when opening them. If you see the alert message, click the **Yes** button. An **"upgrade successful"** alert as shown below may also appear. If you see the alert below, all that you need to do is click the **Continue** button.

Contacting IconLogic

Web: **www.iconlogic.com** | Phone: **888.812.4827** | Email: **ksiegel@iconlogic.com**

ix

Notes

iCONLOGiC

"Skills and Drills" Learning

Rank Your Skills

Before starting this book, complete the skills assessment on the next page.

Skills Assessment

How this assessment works

Below you will find 10 course objectives for *TechSmith Camtasia 2023: The Essentials*. **Before starting the book:** Review each objective and rank your skills using the scale next to each objective. A rank of ① means **No Confidence** in the skill. A rank of ⑤ means **Total Confidence**. After you've completed this assessment, go through the entire book. **After finishing the book:** Review each objective and rank your skills now that you've completed the book. Most people see dramatic improvements in the second assessment after completing the lessons in this book.

Before-Class Skills Assessment

1.	I can add media to the Media Bin.	①	②	③	④	⑤
2.	I can add a Quiz to a Project.	①	②	③	④	⑤
3.	I can create Captions.	①	②	③	④	⑤
4.	I can export Camtasia projects as HTML5.	①	②	③	④	⑤
5.	I can record voiceover audio within Camtasia.	①	②	③	④	⑤
6.	I can add hotspots that jump to markers.	①	②	③	④	⑤
7.	I can create a custom animation.	①	②	③	④	⑤
8.	I can use Corner Pin Mode.	①	②	③	④	⑤
9.	I can export a LMS-ready zipped package.	①	②	③	④	⑤
10.	I can record screen actions using the Camtasia Recorder.	①	②	③	④	⑤

After-Class Skills Assessment

1.	I can add media to the Media Bin.	①	②	③	④	⑤
2.	I can add a Quiz to a Project.	①	②	③	④	⑤
3.	I can create Captions.	①	②	③	④	⑤
4.	I can export Camtasia projects as HTML5.	①	②	③	④	⑤
5.	I can record voiceover audio within Camtasia.	①	②	③	④	⑤
6.	I can add hotspots that jump to markers.	①	②	③	④	⑤
7.	I can create a custom animation.	①	②	③	④	⑤
8.	I can use Corner Pin Mode.	①	②	③	④	⑤
9.	I can export a LMS-ready zipped package.	①	②	③	④	⑤
10.	I can record screen actions using the Camtasia Recorder.	①	②	③	④	⑤

IconLogic, Inc.
www.iconlogic.com | ksiegel@iconlogic.com

iCONLOGiC
"Skills and Drills" Learning

Keyboard Shortcuts

Camtasia 2023 is loaded with keyboard shortcuts that make it more efficient to perform common tasks such as adding captions, importing assets to the media bin, and adding animations and effects.

In the pages that follow, I've included screenshots showing all of the available shortcuts. Keep in mind that you can easily customize the default shortcuts.

Mac Keyboard Shortcuts

You will find these shortcuts from within Camtasia by choosing **Camtasia 2021 > Preferences** and clicking **Shortcuts**.

Animations and Effects

Add last used transition:	⇧T
Add custom animation:	⇧A
Jump to next animation:	⌥K
Jump to previous animation:	⇧K

Canvas Options

Zoom in on canvas:	⌘=
Zoom out on canvas:	⌘-
Preview media outside of group:	⇧⌘G
Pan to here:	^⌘Z
Scale to Fit:	⌥⌘F
Pan and scale to 200%:	^⌘4
Pan and scale to 100%:	^⌘3
Pan and scale to 50%:	^⌘2
Pan and scale to 25%:	^⌘1

Captions

Add captions:	⇧C

Library Options

Add timeline selection to Library:	⌥⌘A

Marker and Quiz Options

Add marker:	⇧M
Show/Hide marker view:	^M
Next marker:	^]
Previous marker:	^[
Extend selection to next marker:	^⇧]
Extend selection to previous marker:	^⇧[
Add quiz:	⇧Q
Show/Hide quiz view:	^Q
Next quiz:	^0
Previous quiz:	^9

Program Options

Show/hide tools panel:	⌘1
Show/hide properties panel:	⌘2
Open media tab:	B
Open favorites tab:	F
Open library tab:	R
Open annotation tab:	N
Open transition tab:	T
Open behaviors tab:	O
Open animations tab:	A
Open cursor effects tab:	U
Open voice narration tab:	V
Open interactivity tab:	I
Open audio effects tab:	D
Open visual effects tab:	X
Open gesture effects tab:	G
Import package:	^⇧P
Export package:	^⇧E

Project Options

Import media:	⌘I
Export frame as:	^F
Export Frame at Playhead:	^⇧F
Export:	⌘E

Recorder Options

Start/pause recording:	⇧⌘2
Stop recording:	⌥⌘2

Timeline Editing

Group:	⌘G
Ungroup:	⌘U
Silence audio:	⌥S
Restore audio:	⌥R
Split selected media:	⌘T
Split all:	⇧⌘T
Stitch selected media:	⌥⌘I
Add annotation:	⇧N
Add placeholder:	P
Duration:	^D

Timeline Navigation

Return playhead:	⌃⌥Space
Previous clip:	⌃,
Next clip:	⌃.
Step backward:	,
Step forward:	.
Zoom in:	⇧⌘=
Zoom out:	⇧⌘-
Zoom to fit:	⇧⌘0
Zoom to max:	⇧⌘9
Zoom to selection:	⇧⌘8
Move playhead to beginning:	⌘↵
Move playhead to end:	⇧⌘↵
Extend selection to next clip:	⌥⇧⌘.
Extend selection to previous clip:	⌥⇧⌘,
Extend selection range right:	⇧.
Extend selection range left:	⇧,
Increase track heights:	⌥=
Decrease track heights:	⌥-
Detach/Attach timeline:	⌘3
Open group:	⌃⇧G

PC Keyboard Shortcuts

You will find these shortcuts from within Camtasia by choosing **Edit > Preferences** and clicking **Shortcuts**.

Animations and Effects

Add last used transition	Shift+T
Add custom animation	Shift+A
Jump to next animation	Alt+K
Jump to previous animation	Shift+K
Start/stop narration recording	Ctrl+Shift+V

Canvas Options

Zoom in on canvas	Ctrl+=
Zoom out on canvas	Ctrl+-
Enable/disable canvas snapping	Ctrl+;

Program Options

Show/hide tools panel	Ctrl+1
Show/hide properties panel	Ctrl+2
Attach/detach Timeline	Ctrl+3
Open media tab	B
Open library tab	R
Open favorites tab	F
Open annotations tab	N
Open transitions tab	T
Open behaviors tab	O
Open animations tab	A
Open cursor effects tab	U
Open voice narration tab	V
Open audio effects tab	D
Open visual effects tab	L
Open interactivity tab	I
Open captions tab	C
Launch preferences dialog	Ctrl+,
Launch recorder	Ctrl+R
Import Package	Ctrl+Shift+P
Export Package	Ctrl+Shift+E

Project Options

Import into media bin	Ctrl+I
Export frame as	Ctrl+F
Add exported frame to playhead	Ctrl+Shift+F
Produce/share production wizard	Ctrl+P
Silence audio	Shift+S

Timeline Editing

Group	Ctrl+G
Ungroup	Ctrl+U
Open group	Ctrl+Shift+G
Close group	Ctrl+Shift+U
Split selected media	S
Split all tracks at playhead	Ctrl+Shift+S
Stitch selected media	Ctrl+Alt+I
Add annotation	Shift+N
Extend frame	Shift+E
Deselect all	Ctrl+D
Ripple delete	Ctrl+Backspace
Add Placeholder	P
Convert to Placeholder	Ctrl+Alt+P

Library Options

Import to library	Add Shortcut
Add selection to library	Ctrl+Shift+A

NOTES

Timeline Navigation

Return playhead	Ctrl+Alt+M
Move playhead to previous clip	Ctrl+Alt+,
Move playhead to next clip	Ctrl+Alt+.
Step backward on timeline	,
Step forward on timeline	.
Zoom in	Ctrl+Shift+=
Zoom out	Ctrl+Shift+-
Zoom to fit	Ctrl+Shift+7
Zoom to max	Ctrl+Shift+9
Zoom to selection	Ctrl+Shift+8
Jump to beginning of timeline	Ctrl+Home
Jump to end of timeline	Ctrl+End
Extend selection to next clip	Ctrl+Alt+Shift+Right
Extend selection to previous clip	Ctrl+Alt+Shift+Left
Extend selection range left	Shift+,
Extend selection range right	Shift+.
Increase track heights	Alt+=
Decrease track heights	Alt+-
Extend selection to timeline beginning	Ctrl+Shift+Home
Extend selection to timeline end	Ctrl+Shift+End
Select succeeding media	Alt+Right
Select preceding media	Alt+Left

Captions

Add caption	Shift+C
Increase caption duration	Ctrl+Alt+]
Decrease caption duration	Ctrl+Alt+[

Marker and Quiz Options

Add marker	Shift+M
Add quiz	Shift+Q
Show/hide marker view	Ctrl+M
Show/hide quiz view	Ctrl+Q
Next marker	Ctrl+]
Previous marker	Ctrl+[
Select next marker	Ctrl+Shift+]
Select previous marker	Ctrl+Shift+[
Next quiz	Ctrl+0
Previous quiz	Ctrl+9

iCONLOGiC

"Skills and Drills" Learning

Preface

In This Module You Will Learn About:

Planning eLearning Lessons

If you want to create eLearning, Camtasia is an essential development tool. However, if your goal is effective and relevant eLearning, consider the following:

☐ **Why are you creating an eLearning course?** You might be surprised by the number of people who start Camtasia and immediately begin creating content. This kind of development process might be well intentioned, but you really need to map out the entire course, including the way you are going to track learner comprehension (if that's important to you). During the initial planning and mapping process, you might conclude that your course isn't appropriate for eLearning and decide upon a different delivery method for the content.

☐ **Who is your audience?** The way children learn is different from adults. For instance, children need praise and encouragement during the learning process; however, adult learners might find such praise and encouragement annoying. Also, you need to know if the learner already has foundational knowledge or are new to the topic. The answer to that question can dramatically alter the direction of the course content.

☐ **What exactly are you teaching, and is it appropriate for eLearning?** Not every lesson in an instructor-led course can be effectively re-tooled for eLearning. For instance, if a course relies on breakout groups, group discussion, or collaborative work, those aspects of the course cannot easily be included in Camtasia. Keep in mind that eLearners usually work independently and have little or no live interaction with others.

☐ **Does your project need closed captions?** If the answer is yes, you should budget approximately 10-15 percent more time to create the closed captions in Camtasia.

☐ **Do you want your projects to contain images, videos, and background music?** If so, where will you find the media assets? If you find assets online, be aware that there are likely usage restrictions. You will learn how to import assets beginning on page 38. You will learn that you can add your own assets and that Camtasia includes a robust number of free assets in the Library. In addition, there are royalty-free assets available via a subscription plan to TechSmith

☐ **Do you need a project template?** You will learn about templates beginning on page 171. If you are required to use a template, are you going to create the template or is it being provided to you?

☐ **Will there be annotations (written instructions and descriptions)?** You will learn how to add annotations beginning on page 64. While annotations are easy to insert, who will write the content contained within the annotations? This role is typically filled by a technical writer/technical communicator.

☐ **Is your course soft skills, or is it a software video demonstration?** Soft skills courses typically teach a life skill such as conflict resolution, onboarding, or interacting with people. Video demonstrations are typically computer screen recordings. You will learn about recording your screen on page 20. If your goal is to create soft skills training, does it make sense to create most of the content in Microsoft PowerPoint and then import the presentation into Camtasia? Given how strong PowerPoint is as a presentation tool, I would encourage you to go the PowerPoint route. There are lessons on importing PowerPoint into Camtasia beginning on page 148.

If you're creating a video demonstration, has someone already created a step-by-step script needed to capture that correct steps/processes? You'll learn about scripts on page 20

eLearning Development Phases

The infographic below offers you a visual guide to the eLearning development process and phases.

A larger version of the graphic can be downloaded from www.iconlogic.com/skills-drills-workbooks/elearning-resources.html. You can also use the camera on your mobile device to scan the code at the right for direct access to the image.

eLearning Development Phases

1. DISCOVERY
Meet with the client. Find out **what they want** in an ideal eLearning course. Who is the **audience**? Define a course **mission statement** for the course in general. You'll also need a mission statement for each lesson in the course. Will the course require **accessibility**? **Audio**? Will it need to be **localized**? What kind of **hardware** will students be using to access the course?

2. DESIGN
Which tool will you be using to develop the content (**Camtasia, Captivate, Presenter, Storyline**, or perhaps a combination of a couple tools)? **Instructional design**, a **graphical treatment**, and **navigational choices** are now made and implemented.

3. WRITING and/or STORYBOARDING
Now that you have chosen a production tool and decided the overall design of the course, you'll need to **plot out the flow** of the course and **write a script and/or a storyboard**. If the course includes voiceover audio, you'll need a separate (and different) script for that.

4. PRODUCTION

Now it's time to get busy with the **development work** in the selected tool. This includes everything right up to the point of publishing. You'll also **beta test** the lessons in this phase as they are completed.

5. CLIENT APPROVAL
You're almost there! But, before project completion, you'll need to get your **client's approval**. Depending upon how this goes, **you may need to repeat parts of steps two, three, and four**.

6. PUBLISHING and IMPLEMENTATION

This includes not only **publishing locally**, but uploading the content to a **web server** or **LMS (SCORM or AICC)**. Be sure to allow time to work out bugs in this phase.

7. MAINTENANCE
You did a great job! But sometimes changes and updates are necessary. This phase includes **making updates** to the content and **re-posting to the LMS or web server**.

Brought to you by:
iCONLOGiC
www.iconlogic.com

NOTES

Camtasia Production Times (Level of Effort)

When I say production time, I'm referring to the actual time you will spend adding content to the Media Bin, adding that content to the Timeline, adding animations, annotations, etc. It may sound like common sense, but the longer the play time for your videos, the longer it will typically take for you to produce them in Camtasia.

Many new eLearning developers underestimate the number of hours needed to produce eLearning. Consider the following guide.

Project Size	Number of Production Hours
Small Videos (1-3 minutes of play time)	1-6 hours
Medium Videos (4-6 minutes)	8-12 hours
Long Videos (7-10 minutes)	14-20 hours
Extra-Long Videos (more than 10 minutes)	Consider splitting videos this large into smaller Camtasia projects.

Project Size and Display Resolution

Several years ago, monitors were small and display resolutions low and a display resolution of 800 x 600 pixels was common. If you developed eLearning content for a small display, a Camtasia canvas size of 640 x 480 worked well.

A few years later, 1024 x 768 was the standard display resolution, resulting in typical Camtasia projects sized to 800 x 600. Today, a common desktop screen resolution is higher than 1366 x 768.

What's the ideal size for a Camtasia project? Unfortunately, there isn't one absolute answer. The width and height of a software demonstration you record depends largely on the size of your display, your display resolution, and the software you're recording (some software cannot be resized and may need to take up the entire screen).

Video cards and display sizes vary from computer to computer. I like my Camtasia courses and screen recordings to look consistent, so I always use the same computer, display resolution, Camtasia project template, Camtasia project size, and screen recording size.

In the image at the right, notice the suggested Canvas Dimensions available in Camtasia's Project Settings.

According to TechSmith, if you are creating content for learners on Instagram, consider a Canvas size of 640 x 640. FaceBook video? Think 820 x 462. YouTube? Consider a project size of 1280 x 720.

If your target audience uses mobile devices or widescreen displays, widescreen dimensions such as 720p work well.

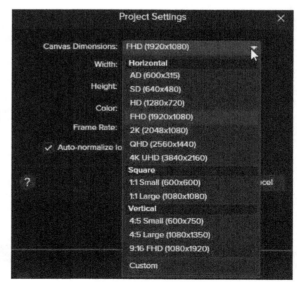

Design Best Practices

Much of what you do in Camtasia will feel similar to what you can do in Microsoft PowerPoint. If you've used PowerPoint, you are familiar with adding objects to a slide. In Camtasia, you add objects to the Canvas and use the Timeline to control when those objects are seen by the learner. Unlike PowerPoint, which can contain hundreds of slides, there is only one Canvas in Camtasia, and only one Timeline.

You don't have to be a seasoned designer to produce beautiful and effective Camtasia projects. Here are a few tips to get you started:

- ❑ If you're creating the content in PowerPoint, there are occasions when a bulleted list is the best way to convey an idea. Although PowerPoint uses a bulleted approach to information by default, you do not have to use that format in eLearning.

- ❑ Try splitting the bullets into separate slides with a single image to illustrate each point, or forgo the text and replace it with a chart, diagram, or other informative/interesting image.

- ❑ It is not necessary to have every bit of information you cover on the screen at one time. Encourage your audience to listen and, if necessary, take notes based on what you say, not what is shown on the screen.

- ❑ Few learners are impressed with how many moving, colorful objects each slide contains. When it comes to eLearning, the old saying "content is King" has never been more appropriate. Ensure each of your screens contains relevant, need-to-know information and that the information is presented as clutter-free as possible.

- ❑ Consider taking more of a photographic approach to the images you use. You can easily find stock photographs on the web using any one of a number of pay-for-use websites. There are many free sites, but keep in mind that to save time and frustration (and improve on the selection and quality), you might want to set aside a budget to pay for images.

Fonts and eLearning

The most important thing about eLearning is solid content. But could you be inadvertently making your content harder to read and understand by using the wrong fonts? Is good font selection really important? Read on to discover the many surprising ways fonts can affect your content.

Some Fonts Read Better On-Screen

eCommerce Consultant **Dr. Ralph F. Wilson** did a study to determine if serif fonts (fonts with little lines on the tops and bottoms of characters, such as Times New Roman) or sans serif fonts (those without lines, such as Arial) were more suited to being read on computer monitors. His study concluded that although Times New Roman is easily read in printed materials, the lower resolution of monitors (72 dots per inch (dpi) versus 180 dpi or higher) makes it much more difficult to read in digital format. Times New Roman 12 pt was pitted against Arial 12 pt with respondents finding the sans serif Arial font more readable at a rate of two to one.

Lorem ipsum frangali puttuto rigali fortuitous confulence magficati alorem. Lorem ipsum frangali puttuto rigali fortuitous confulence magficati alorem.	Lorem ipsum frangali puttuto rigali fortuitous confulence magficati alorem. Lorem ipsum frangali puttuto rigali fortuitous confulence magficati alorem.
Times New Roman 12 pt	Arial 12 pt
520	1123
32%	68%

Source: http://www.practicalecommerce.com/articles/100159-html-email-fonts

Wilson also tested the readability of Arial versus Verdana on computer screens and found that in font sizes greater than 10 pt, Arial was more readable, whereas Verdana was more readable in font sizes 10 pt and smaller.

So should you stop using Times New Roman in your eLearning lessons? Not completely. For instance, you can use Times New Roman for text content that is not expected to be read quickly.

Some Fonts Increase Trust

A study by **Sharath Sasidharan** and **Ganga Dhanesh** for the Association of Information Systems found that typography can affect trust in eCommerce. The study found that to instill trust in online consumers, you should keep it simple: "To the extent possible, particularly for websites that need to engage in financial transactions or collect personal information from their users, the dominant typeface used to present text material should be a serif or sans serif font such as Times New Roman or Arial."

If you feel your eLearning content will be presented to a skeptical audience (or one you've never worked with before), dazzling them with fancy fonts may not be the way to go. You can use fancy fonts from time to time to break up the monotony of a dry lesson but use such nonstandard fonts sparingly. Use the fancy fonts for headings or as accents, but not for the bulk of your text.

The Readability of Fonts Affects Participation

A University of Michigan study on typecase in instructions found that the ease with which a font in instructional material is read can have an impact on the perceived skill level needed to complete a task.

The study found that if directions are presented in a font that is deemed more difficult to read, the task will be viewed as being difficult, taking a long time to complete, and perhaps, not even worth trying.The also suggests that it is not a good idea create Camtasia annotations using the Times New Roman font because it could make the content more difficult to process and become overwhelming, especially to beginners.

Popular eLearning Fonts

I ran a poll where I asked developers which fonts they tended to use in eLearning. Here is a list of the most popular fonts:

- ☐ Verdana
- ☐ Helvetica
- ☐ Arial
- ☐ Calibri
- ☐ Times
- ☐ Palatino
- ☐ Times New Roman
- ☐ Century Schoolbook (for print)

NOTES

Fonts and Personas

Camtasia's default font is Montserrat and it can be changed easily using the Properties panel. If you are creating eLearning for business professionals, you might want to use a font that is different from one you would use if you were creating eLearning for high school students. But what font would you use if you want to convey a feeling of happiness? Formality? Cuddliness?

In a study (funded by Microsoft) by **A. Dawn Shaikh**, **Barbara S. Chaparro**, and **Doug Fox**, the perceived personality traits of fonts are categorized. The table below shows the top three fonts for each personality objective.

	Top Three		
Stable	TNR	Arial	Cambria
Flexible	Kristen	Gigi	Rage Italic
Conformist	Courier New	TNR	Arial
Polite	Monotype Corsiva	TNR	Cambria
Mature	TNR	Courier New	Cambria
Formal	TNR	Monotype Corsiva	Georgia
Assertive	Impact	Rockwell Xbold	Georgia
Practical	Georgia	TNR	Cambria
Creative	Gigi	Kristen	Rage Italic
Happy	Kristen	Gigi	Comic Sans
Exciting	Gigi	Kristen	Rage Italic
Attractive	Monotype Corsiva	Rage Italic	Gigi
Elegant	Monotype Corsiva	Rage Italic	Gigi
Cuddly	Kristen	Gigi	Comic Sans
Feminine	Gigi	Monotype Corsiva	Kristen
Unstable	Gigi	Kristen	Rage Italic
Rigid	Impact	Courier New	Agency FB
Rebel	Gigi	Kristen	Rage Italic
Rude	Impact	Rockwell Xbold	Agency FB
Youthful	Kristen	Gigi	Comic Sans
Casual	Kristen	Comic Sans	Gigi
Passive	Kristen	Gigi	Comic Sans
Impractical	Gigi	Rage Italic	Kristen
Unimaginative	Courier New	Arial	Consolas
Sad	Impact	Courier New	Agency FB
Dull	Courier New	Consolas	Verdana
Unattractive	Impact	Courier New	Rockwell Xbold
Plain	Courier New	Impact	Rockwell Xbold
Coarse	Impact	Rockwell Xbold	Courier New
Masculine	Impact	Rockwell Xbold	Courier New

Source: http://www.usabilitynews.org

iCONLOGiC

"Skills and Drills" Learning

Module 1: Exploring Camtasia

In This Module You Will Learn About:

And You Will Learn To:

The Camtasia Interface

During these first few guided activities, I'd like to give you a chance to familiarize yourself with Camtasia's workspace. Specifically, you'll start Camtasia, access the Getting Started project, open a project from the **Camtasia2023Data** folder, and poke around Camtasia's interface a bit.

Guided Activity 1: Explore a Completed Camtasia Project

1. Start Camtasia 2023.

    The **Home screen** opens. (If you do not see the Home Window, choose **File > Home** to open it.)

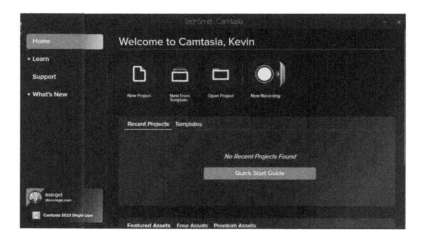

Note: If you have not yet downloaded this book's support assets (also known as Data Files), turn to the **About This Book** section at the beginning of this book and work through the **Download and Extract the Data Files** activity on page viii.

2. Open a project from the Camtasia2023Data folder.

    ❑ from the options at the left on the **Home** screen, click **Home**

    ❑ from beneath the heading "Welcome to Camtasia," click the **Open Project** icon

    The **Open** dialog box appears.

    ❑ navigate to the **Camtasia2023Data** folder

    ❑ open the **Projects** folder and then open the **Demo.tscproj** folder

    ❑ open the **Demo.tscproj** file

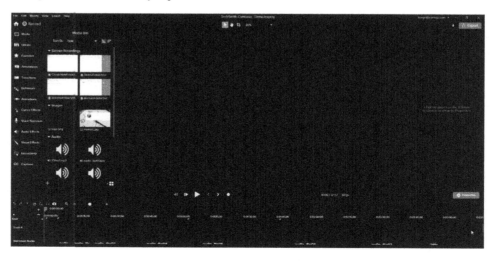

3. View the Voice Narration tool.

   ☐ choose **View > Tools > Voice Narration**

   The Voice Narration features open. This area is used to record voice narration. You will learn to record voiceover audio beginning on page 92.

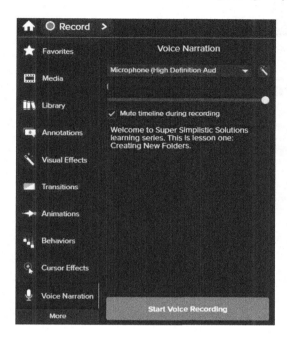

   Note: You can access all of the tools, such as Voice Narration, from the list of tools at the left. Depending upon the size of your screen, you may need to click **More** at the bottom of the list to see all of the tools.

4. Display the Annotations.

   ☐ from the list of tools at the left, click **Annotations**

   There are six Annotation categories. Annotations are used to focus the learner's attention to specific areas of a video. Annotation types include Callouts, Arrows & Lines, Shapes, Blur & Highlight, Sketch Motion, and Keystroke callouts. You will learn to work with Annotations beginning on page 64.

NOTES

5. Display the Transitions.

☐ from the list of tools at the left, click **Transitions**

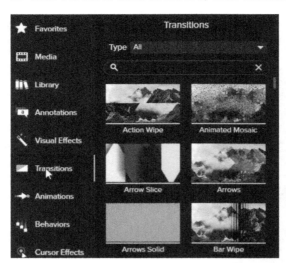

Transitions give you the ability to move from one part of your lesson to another using professional animation effects. You'll learn how to add Transitions to a project beginning on page 77.

Next you will explore the Media Bin and the Library.

The Media Bin and Library

The Media Bin and Library provide access to media such as images, videos, and audio that can be added to the Camtasia Timeline.

Every Camtasia project has its own Media Bin, and it is empty by default. As you import assets into the Media Bin, those assets can be added directly to the Canvas, the Timeline, or the Library. There is no limit to how many assets you can add to the Media Bin, but the bin cannot be shared or opened by other Camtasia projects.

The Library comes preloaded with dozens of free assets provided by TechSmith, including animations, icons, and music. Unlike the Media Bin, Library assets are available to any Camtasia project on your computer. And Library assets can be exported and shared with other Camtasia developers on your team.

Guided Activity 2: Explore the Media Bin and Library

1. Ensure that the **Demo** project is open.

2. View the Media Bin.

   ☐ from the list of tools at the left, click **Media**

   There are several assets in this project's Media Bin, including screen recordings, images, and audio.

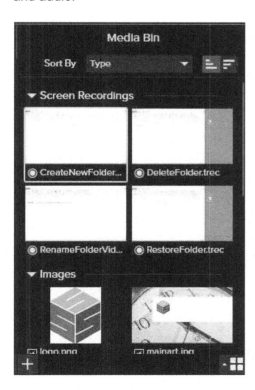

The default view for the Media Bin is Thumbnails, which is nice if you want a decent-sized preview of the Media Bin assets. However, many developers prefer the organized look and feel of the Details view.

NOTES

3. Change the Media Bin view from Thumbnails to Details.

☐ at the bottom right of the **Media Bin,** click the **Change Media Bin view** icon

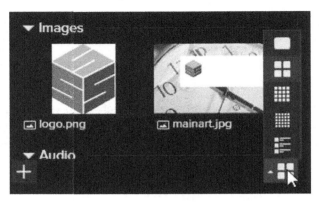

☐ click the **Details** icon

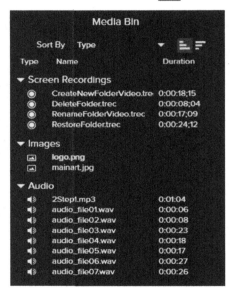

4. Change the Media Bin view from Details back to tiled thumbnails.

☐ at the bottom right of the **Media Bin**, click the **Change Media Bin view** icon

☐ click the **tiled thumbnails** icon

You will learn how to add assets to the Media Bin beginning on page 39.

5. View the Library.

☐ from the list of tools at the left, click **Library**

The Library takes the space previously occupied by the Media Bin. By default, there are several folders within the Library containing images, animations, and audio files. You can create your own folders and import your own assets into the Library. Also, there is a link at the bottom of the Library labeled **Download more assets.** TechSmith offers a subscription service that provides thousands of royalty-free videos, images, and audio files you can use in your Camtasia project. You won't need the subscription service to complete this book because you'll be using the free assets currently in the Library or within the Camtasia2023Data folder. However, once you start creating your own projects and need assets such as videos, images, or icons, the subscription may prove invaluable.

6. Preview a Library asset.

   ❑ from the Library drop-down menu, choose **Camtasia 2023** (if necessary)

   ❑ on the **Library**, expand (open) the **Audio** folder

   ❑ double-click any of the audio assets

   A preview window opens, and assuming you have speakers or a headset, you will hear the music.

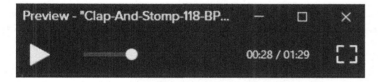

7. Close the audio preview window.

   You will learn how to add Library audio assets to the Timeline later.

The Canvas and Timeline

The Canvas, also known as the Stage, offers an excellent way to position screen elements and preview the project as you're working. As you preview a project on the Canvas, you'll be able to use the Timeline to keep track of and control the media.

The Timeline is at the bottom of the Camtasia window. The Timeline is used to control the timing of objects added to the Canvas. For instance, using the Timeline, you can force objects such as images or videos to appear at the same time, or you can force one object to appear as another goes away.

Guided Activity 3: Use the Canvas to Preview a Project

1. Ensure that the **Demo** project is open.

2. Preview the project.

   ☐ below the **Canvas**, click **Play** icon

As the preview plays on the Canvas, notice that an object moves across the Timeline. The object is known as the Playhead. The Playhead includes a thin vertical line and a green and a red square, which you will learn about later. The Playhead and thin line show you where the Canvas preview is at any specific point in time. You will learn to work with the Timeline as you work through the lessons in this book.

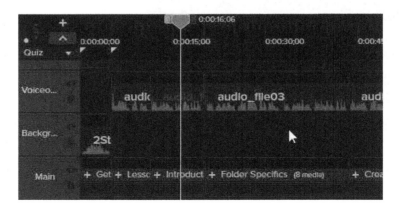

3. Detach the Canvas.

   ☐ choose **View > Canvas > Detach Canvas** (you can also find the Detach Canvas option in the **Canvas Options** drop-down menu located just above the Canvas)

Click the menu located just above the **Canvas** to find the **Detach Canvas** menu item.

With the canvas detached, you can now position it anywhere on your screen or, if you're using multiple monitors, drag it from one screen to the other.

4. Explore Full Screen Mode.

    ☐ with the Canvas detached, click the **Full Screen** icon (it's in the lower right of the detached Canvas)

    While in Full Screen mode, you can see the lesson but not the Camtasia interface.

5. Exit Full Screen mode.

    ☐ press [**esc**] on your keyboard

6. Attach the Canvas.

    ☐ choose **View > Canvas > Attach Canvas**

    The Canvas reattaches itself to the Editor.

NOTES

7. Use a keyboard shortcut to Zoom closer and farther away from the Canvas.

    ❑ PC users, press [**ctrl**] [=] a few times to zoom closer to the Canvas
    Mac users, press [**command**] [=] a few times to zoom closer to the Canvas

    ❑ PC users, press [**ctrl**] [-] a few times to zoom away from the Canvas
    Mac users, press [**command**] [-] a few times to zoom away from the Canvas

8. Modify the Canvas zooming keyboard shortcuts.

    ❑ PC users, choose **Edit > Preferences**
    Mac users, choose **Camtasia 2023 > Preferences**

    The Preferences dialog box opens.

    ❑ select the **Shortcuts** tab

    ❑ select **Canvas Options**

    ❑ to the right of **Zoom in on Canvas**, click the current keyboard shortcut

    ❑ PC users, replace the shortcut with [**ctrl**] [**shift**] [=]
    Mac users, replace the shortcut with [**shift**] [**command**] [=]

Zoom in on canvas	Ctrl+Shift+=

Zoom in on canvas:	⇧⌘= ↺

    ❑ PC users, click the **OK** button; Mac users, close the Shortcuts dialog box

9. Test the modified keyboard shortcuts.

    ❑ PC users, press [**ctrl**] [**shift**] [+] a few times to zoom closer to the Canvas;
    Mac users, press [**command**] [**shift**] [+] a few times to zoom closer to the Canvas

    ❑ PC users, press [**ctrl**] [-] a few times to zoom away from the Canvas;
    Mac users, press [**command**] [-] to zoom away from the Canvas

10. Restore the keyboard shortcuts to their defaults.

    ❑ PC users, choose **Edit > Preferences**;
    Mac users, choose **Camtasia 2023 > Preferences**

    The Preferences dialog box reopens.

    ❑ select the **Shortcuts** tab

    ❑ PC users, click the **Restore defaults** button
    Mac users, from the **Shortcut Set** menu, choose **TechSmith Camtasia Default**

    ❑ PC users, click the **OK** button;
    Mac users, close the Shortcuts dialog box

11. Exit Camtasia.

    ❑ PC users choose **File > Exit**; Mac users, choose **Camtasia 2023 > Quit**

    There is no need to save any changes made to the Demo project (if prompted).

iCONLOGiC

"Skills and Drills" Learning

Module 2: Recording Videos

In This Module You Will Learn About:

And You Will Learn To:

Rehearsals

During this module, you are going to learn how to use Camtasia to record a series of steps you perform on your computer. You will be using either Notepad (PC) or Text Edit (Mac) during the next few activities. The process of starting either Notepad or TextEdit varies slightly depending on your operating system.

> **Note:** If you are using Windows, click **Start** or the **Windows** button, type **notepad**, and then press **[enter]** to start Notepad.

> If you are using a Mac, from **Finder**, choose **Go > Applications**. Double click TextEdit to open it. On the TextEdit dialog box, click **New Document** button to create a new TextEdit document (if necessary).

The Scenario

You have been hired to create an eLearning course that teaches new employees at your company how to use **Notepad** (if you're using Camtasia for Windows) or **TextEdit** (if you're using Camtasia for the Mac). One of the lessons you plan to record using Camtasia includes how to change the page orientation within Notepad or TextEdit.

Step-by-Step Recording Script

Here is a detailed, step-by-step set of instructions you would typically write yourself or receive from a technical/script writer, the Subject Matter Expert (SME), or the instructional designer. As the Camtasia expert, your job will be to perform each step exactly as written below in either Notepad or TextEdit.

1. Start either Notepad or TextEdit. (If you are using TextEdit, create a new, blank document after starting the program.)
2. From within Notepad or TextEdit, click the **File** menu.
3. Click the **Page Setup** menu item.
4. Click the **Landscape** orientation button.
5. Click the **OK** button.
6. Click the **File** menu.
7. Click the **Page Setup** menu item.
8. Click the **Portrait** orientation button.
9. Click the **OK** button.

The script above sounds simple. However, you will not know what kind of problems you are going to get into unless you rehearse the script prior to recording the process with Camtasia.

Let's run a rehearsal, just as if you were a big-time movie director and you were in charge of a blockbuster movie.

Places everyone, *and quiet on the set.*

Guided Activity 4: Rehearse a Script

1. Start Notepad (PC) or TextEdit (Mac).

 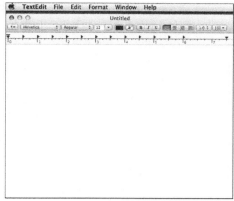

Note: In the images on this page, Notepad from Windows 10 is pictured at the left; TextEdit is at the right.

While Notepad in Windows 11 looks a bit different than the classic version of Notepad, the functionality between the Windows 10 and Windows 11 version is the same as it relates to the activities in this module.

2. Rehearse the script.

   ❏ using **Notepad** or **TextEdit** (not Camtasia), click the **File** menu

   ❏ click the **Page Setup** menu item

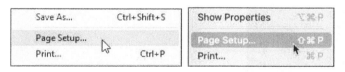

   ❏ from the **Orientation** area, click **Landscape**

   ❏ click the **OK** button
   ❏ click the **File** menu
   ❏ click the **Page Setup** menu item
   ❏ click the **Portrait** orientation button
   ❏ click the **OK** button

The script worked perfectly, and there were no surprises. Next, you will work through the same steps again. Only this time, you will record every click with the Camtasia Recorder. As you click, the recorder creates a video of the entire process. That video will be used in the Camtasia editor and serve as the foundation for an eLearning course you will develop during the activities in this book.

NOTES

Recording Screen Actions

When recording screen actions using Camtasia, pretend you are using a video recorder or your mobile device to create a movie. You're both the director and the producer. During the recording process, everything you do is captured. Every delay, every good click, bad click, right-click, double-click... everything is recorded. If you move your mouse too fast and race through the script, the resulting video will play back the cursor speed in real time. If you move your mouse too slow, your learners will tear their collective hairs out as they watch your mouse creep across the screen.

In the steps that follow, you'll select a recording area and then record the process of changing the Page Orientation in Notepad or TextEdit.

> **Note:** While Camtasia is similar on the Mac and PC, recording screen actions is different. On the PC, there's a separate program used for recording videos called Camtasia Recorder. On the Mac, you can record with Camtasia, but there isn't a standalone Recorder program. Because recording videos on the two operating systems is so different, I'm showing the two processes separately. PC users, your activities appear below. Mac users, skip ahead to page 28.

Guided Activity 5: Specify a PC Recording Screen and Size

1. Start the Camtasia 2023.

2. Start the Camtasia Recorder 2023 tool.

   ☐ from the **Home** area of the Camtasia Home window, click **New Recording**

The Camtasia Recorder opens. There is a large green, dashed recording area that is likely the size of your screen. There is also a control panel containing five sections: Screen, Web Cam, Microphone, System Audio, and a red Start recording button.

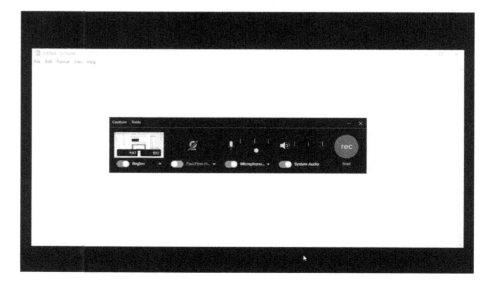

3. Select the screen to record.

   ❏ if necessary, click the slider in the **screen** area to allow Camtasia to record the screen

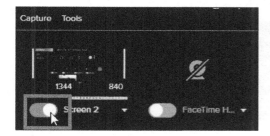

Note: The sliders on the Recorder are toggles. Each option is either on or off. Green means the option is enabled; gray means the option is disabled.

   ❏ from the **Screen** drop-down menu, select the screen containing Notepad

The options you see in the menu are dependent upon the number of screens physically connected to your computer. In the image below, I have two screens. My Notepad application is open and positioned on Screen 2.

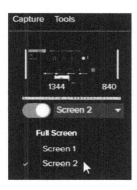

4. Specify the size of the recording area.

   ❏ from the **Screen** drop-down menu, **Horizontal** group, choose **720p (1280x720)**

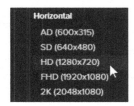

On your screen, the size of the recording area changes to 1280x720 pixels.

Most devices have screens that are wider than they are tall. For that reason, selecting one of the sizes from the Horizontal group makes sense. Between the available sizes, the perfect size is debatable. In my experience, 1280x720 is currently the more common size used by eLearning developers. However, the trend is moving toward larger screen captures, so sizes such as 1080p is gaining in popularity.

5. Disable the Camera, Microphone, and System Audio.

☐ on the Recorder's Control panel, push the slider for the Webcam, Microphone, and System Audio **left** to disable each of the options

Why Disable The Camera?

If you're considering capturing video of yourself, ask yourself this question: "Is my video enhancing the learner experience?" The honest answer will likely be no.

If the answer is yes, then consider the following and perhaps you'll change your mind.

Are you dressed appropriately?

What's behind you? Is there a poster in the background that's inappropriate?

If you look good and the background is great, what about the lighting around you?

What about your camera angle (is the camera pointed straight up your nose)?

While I don't want you to use your webcam at this point, play around with it later. And if you already have awesome videos of yourself, you can import them into Camtasia later (see page 39).

Why Disable The Microphone?

In my experience, audio and video enhance the learner experience. However, using your microphone now, while you're just learning how to use the Camtasia Recorder, isn't such a great idea. Until you're comfortable recording screen actions, you'll likely end up having to replace the audio later. When teamed with the concentration needed to capture quality screen actions, many people tend to talk too fast, too slow, or flub the voice recording.

You'll learn later that it's easy to import, record, and edit audio from within Camtasia (see page 85). However, once you're comfortable recording video demos with Camtasia, absolutely use your microphone to record your voice while creating the video.

Why Disable System Audio?

I usually disable System Audio because there are few sounds my computer makes that I want included in my Camtasia project. However, if I was recording a virtual meeting—via Zoom or WebEx for example—I would enable System audio so that I captured the audio from the meeting.

Guided Activity 6: Create a Software Video Demo on the PC

1. Specify what is to be recorded by Camtasia.

   ❏ on your screen, move and resize the **Notepad** application window as necessary so that the application fits within the 1280x720 Camtasia Recorder capture area

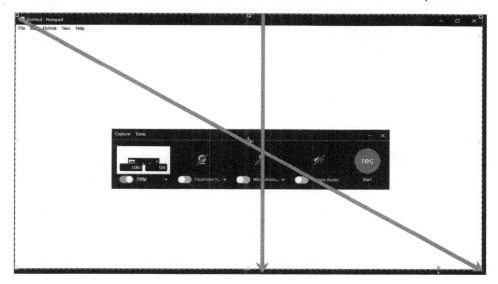

2. Record a software demonstration.

   ❏ on the Camtasia Recorder control panel, click the red **rec** button

   You'll see a three-second countdown.

   ❏ before the counter gets to zero, position your mouse pointer in the **center** of the Notepad window

   After the counter disappears, your every move (and the time it takes you to move) is being recorded.

   ❏ moving steadily (not too fast), move your mouse pointer to the **File** menu

   ❏ click the **Page Setup** menu item

   ❏ from the **Orientation** area, click **Landscape**

   ❏ click the **OK** button

   ❏ click the **File** menu

   ❏ click the **Page Setup** menu item

   ❏ click the **Portrait** orientation button

   ❏ click the **OK** button

3. Stop the recording process.

   ❏ on the Camtasia recorder's control panel, click the **Stop** button

Once you stop the recording process, the main Camtasia interface opens. A new project is created, and the recording is automatically added to the Camtasia Media Bin. The media is also automatically inserted onto the Timeline.

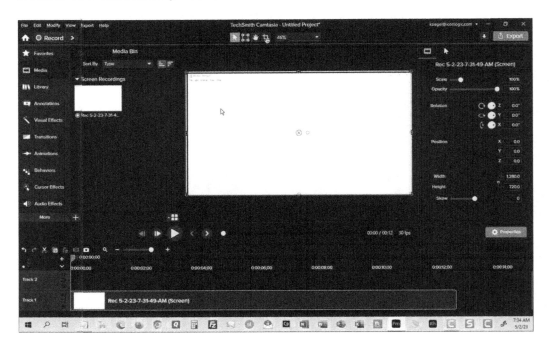

If you'd like to watch the video you recorded, you can use the controls on the Canvas to play and rewind the video as you learned in the last module.

4. View the location of the recording.

   ☐ on the **Media Bin**, right-click the recording and choose **Open File Location**

   The Camtasia folder opens. By default, all of the recordings you create are saved to this folder.

5. Close the window and return to the Camtasia project.

Recording Confidence Check (PC)

1. On the Canvas, Preview the project.

2. If you are happy with the recording, save the project to the **Camtasia2023Data** folder as **My First Recording.**

   When saving, it's a great idea to ensure that **Create standalone project** is selected. When using this option, all of the media assets used in the project are collected and kept together. Creating a standalone project makes it easier to share projects with other Camtasia developers.

3. If you are unhappy with the recording:

   ☐ Delete the recording media from the **Timeline** (right-click > Delete).

   ☐ Delete the recording media from the **Media Bin** (right-click > Delete).

   ☐ From the upper left of the Camtasia window, click the **Record** icon and re-record the software demonstration.

4. Preview the project.

5. If you are happy with the new recording, save the project to the **Camtasia2023Data** folder as **My First Recording.**

6. Exit Camtasia.

7. Exit the Camtasia Recorder.

8. Exit the Notepad application.

   Note: The rest of this module is for Mac users only. PC users, you can skip ahead to the "Adding Media" module which begins on page 37.

NOTES

Guided Activity 7: Set Screen Recording Options on the Mac

1. Start the Camtasia 2023.

2. Change Camtasia's Preferences so that recordings open in the Editor.

   ☐ choose **Camtasia 2023 > Preferences**

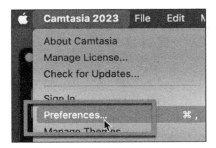

   The Preferences dialog box opens.

   ☐ from the top of the **Preferences** screen, click **Recording**

   ☐ from the **After recording** drop-down menu, choose **Open in Editor** (if necessary)

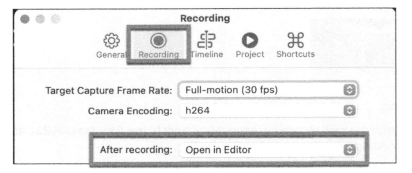

   With the **Open in Editor** option selected, your recording automatically opens in the Camtasia Editor once you stop the recording process.

3. Change the Preferences so that recordings are not automatically deleted.

   ☐ if necessary, remove the check mark from **Delete after**

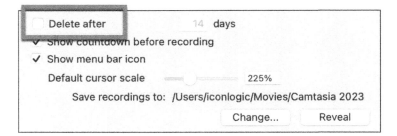

   With **Delete after** disabled, recordings won't be automatically deleted from your computer. Assuming you've backed up your projects and project media, consider manually removing older recordings from the Camtasia 2023 folder monthly.

The remaining **Recording** options should match the image below.

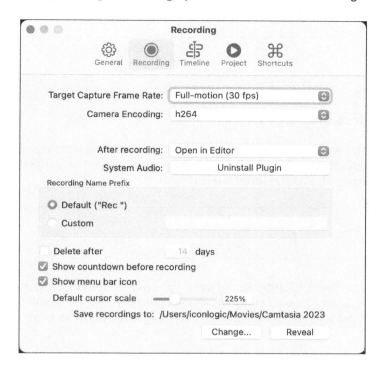

The two most important default Preferences that you did not change are **Target Capture Frame Rate** and **Show countdown before recording**.

By default, recordings are captured at 30 frames-per-second (30 fps). The higher the frame rate, the smoother a recorded video will be. However, when captured at a high frame rate, the file size of a video can be huge, especially if your recording lasts more than a few minutes. If you find that the length of your videos is more than a few minutes, you can experiment with lowering the frame rate prior to recording. This will lower the size of your recording, but could also lower the quality.

Having the **Show countdown before recording** option turned on is a good default. Without this option enabled, the recording process will begin the instant you click the **Start Recording** button... so fast you'll possibly find yourself unprepared and make mistakes while recording.

Note: If your **System Audio** area shows **Install plugin** instead of **Uninstall plugin** as shown above, click the button. When asked **Do you want to install the system Audio Plugin?**, click **Install**.

4. Set a Stop recording Shortcut.

   ☐ from the top of the dialog box, click **Shortcuts**

   ☐ from the list at the left, click **Recorder Options**

From the **Shortcut Set** drop-down menu, choose **TechSmith Camtasia Default**. You can stop the recording process by clicking a stop button on the recorder or use your keyboard.

There are two Recorder shortcuts: **Start/pause** and **Stop**. You can click the shortcut buttons and decide which keyboard keys will Start/pause or Stop the recording.

❒ at the right of **Stop recording**, click the button

The Stop recording button enters edit mode. At this point, you could change the shortcut by pressing a key combination on your keyboard. In the image below, I've temporarily changed the Stop recording shortcut to [**control**] [**E**].

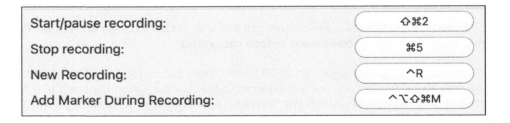

In the image above, notice the highlighted **Reset** icon. Typically the default Stop recording shortcut is fine on the Mac, and I would suggest not changing it. However, if you have played around with different shortcut combinations, click the Reset icon now to restore the shortcut to the default.

Start/pause recording:	⇧⌘2
Stop recording:	⌘5
New Recording:	^R
Add Marker During Recording:	^⌥⇧⌘M

5. Close the Preferences dialog box.

Guided Activity 8: Specify a Mac Recording Screen and Size

1. Ensure that the **TextEdit** application is running.

2. Create a new Camtasia recording.

    ❑ from the **Home** area of the Home window, click **New Recording**

    The Camtasia Recorder opens. There is a large recording area with a green border that is likely the size of your screen. There is also a control panel containing five sections: Screen, Camera, Microphone, System Audio, and a large red Start recording button.

3. Choose a screen to record.

    ❑ if necessary, click the **slider** in the **screen** area to allow Camtasia to record the screen

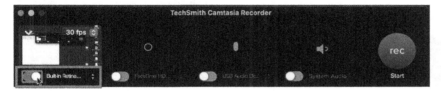

    Note: The sliders on the Recorder are toggles. Each option is either on or off. Green means the option is enabled; gray means the option is disabled.

    ❑ from the **Screen** drop-down menu, select the screen containing **TextEdit**

    The options you see in the menu are dependent upon the number of screens physically connected to your computer. In the image below, I have two screens. **TextEdit** is positioned on my Built-in Retina Display.

4. Specify the size of the recording area.

    ❑ from the **Screen** drop-down menu, **Horizaontal** group, choose **1080p (1920x1080)**

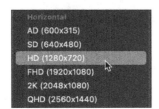

On your screen, the size of the recording area changes to 1920x1080 pixels.

Most devices have screens that are wider than they are tall. For that reason, selecting one of the sizes from the Horizontal group makes sense. Between the available sizes, the perfect size is debatable. In my experience, 1280x720 is currently the more common size used by eLearning developers. However, the trend is moving toward larger screen captures, so sizes such as 1080p is gaining in popularity. And because 1280x720 is likely too small of a capture size on a Mac's Retina Display, you're going with 1920x1080.

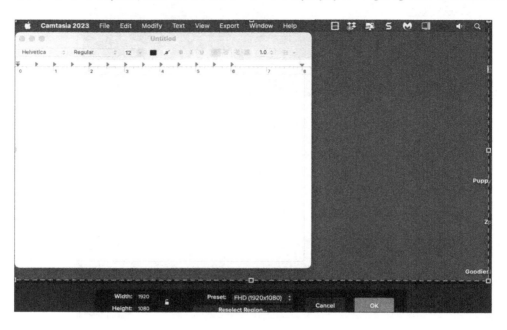

❒ click the **OK** button

5. Select an area of the screen to be recorded.

❒ resize the TextEdit application window as necessary so that both the TextEdit **menu bar** and the TextEdit **application window** fit within the green Camtasia Recording Area

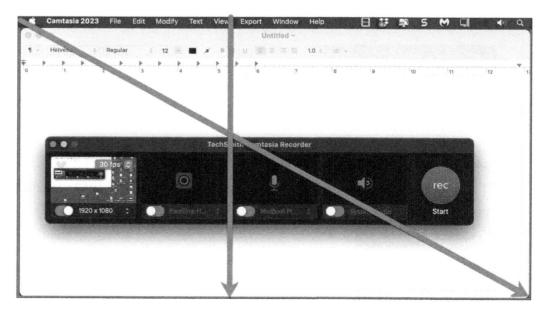

6. Disable the Camera, Microphone, and System Audio.

   ☐ on the Camtasia Recorder, disable your Webcam, Microphone, and System Audio.

Why Disable The Camera?

If you're considering capturing a video of yourself, ask yourself this question: "Is my video enhancing the learner experience?" The honest answer will likely be no.

If the answer is yes, then consider the following and perhaps you'll change your mind.

Are you dressed appropriately?

What's behind you? Is there a poster in the background that's inappropriate?

If you look good and the background is great, what about the lighting around you?

What about your camera angle (is the camera pointed straight up your nose)?

While I discourage you from using your webcam at this point, play around with this feature later. And if you already have awesome videos of yourself created an another program, you can import them into Camtasia later (see page 39).

Why Disable The Microphone?

Audio and video enhance the learner experience. However, using your microphone to record audio now, while you're just learning how to use the Camtasia Recorder, isn't such a great idea. If you're not comfortable recording screen actions, you'll likely end up having to replace the audio later. When teamed with the concentration needed to capture quality screen actions, many people tend to talk too fast, too slow, or flub the recording.

You'll learn later that it's easy to import, record, and edit audio from within Camtasia (see page 85). Once you're comfortable recording video demos, absolutely record yourself talking through the video demo down the road.

Why Disable System Audio?

I usually disable System Audio because there are few sounds my computer makes that I want included in my Camtasia project. However, if I was recording a virtual meeting (via Zoom or WebEx for example), I would enable System audio so that I captured the audio from the meeting.

NOTES

Guided Activity 9: Create a Software Video Demo on the Mac

1. Record a software demonstration.

   ☐ on the Camtasia Recorder, click the red **Start** button

   You'll see a three-second countdown.

   ☐ before the counter gets to zero, position your mouse pointer in the center of the **TextEdit** window and click

   After the counter disappears, your every move (and the time it takes you to move) is being recorded.

   ☐ moving steadily (not too fast), move your mouse pointer to the **File** menu

   ☐ click the **Page Setup** menu item

   ☐ from the **Orientation** area, click **Landscape**

   ☐ click the **OK** button

   ☐ click the **File** menu

   ☐ click the **Page Setup** menu item

   ☐ click the **Portrait** orientation button

   ☐ click the **OK** button

Note: If your stop recording keyboard shortcut does not work, you can force the recording to stop by right-clicking the Camtasia icon on the Dock and choosing Stop Recording.

2. Stop the recording process.

   ☐ on your keyboard, press [**command**] [**5**] (or the shortcut you set up on page 30)

   Once you Stop the recording process, a few things happen in rapid succession. First, the Camtasia Recorder application closes. Second, the Camtasia Editor opens. Third, a new project is created. The recording you created is added to the Camtasia Media Bin and inserted onto the Timeline.

Recording Confidence Check (Mac)

1. On the Canvas, Preview the project.

2. If you are happy with the recording, save the project to the **Camtasia2023Data** folder as **My First Recording.**

   When saving, it's a great idea to ensure that **Create standalone project** is selected. When using this option, all of the media assets used in the project are collected and kept together. Creating a standalone project makes it easier to share projects with other Camtasia developers.

3. If you are unhappy with the recording:

   ☐ Delete the recording media from the **Timeline** (right-click > Delete).

   ☐ Delete the recording media from the **Media Bin** (right-click > Delete).

   ☐ From the upper left of the Camtasia window, click the **Record** icon and re-record the software demonstration.

4. Preview the project.

5. If you are happy with the new recording, save the project to the **Camtasia2023Data** folder as **My First Recording.**

6. On the **Media Bin**, right-click the recording and choose **Reveal in Finder**.

   The Recordings folder opens. By default, all of the recordings you create are saved to this folder.

7. Close the window and return to the Camtasia project.

8. Quit Camtasia.

9. Quit the TextEdit application.

Notes

iCONLOGiC
"Skills and Drills" Learning

Module 3: Adding Media

In This Module You Will Learn About:

And You Will Learn To:

New Projects and Adding Videos

During the first module of this book, you were introduced to the tools that make up Camtasia and explored the Camtasia interface (beginning on page 10). Then you used the Camtasia Recorder to record screen actions (beginning on page 22). Now you'll create a Camtasia project from scratch, set the canvas dimensions, and add media.

Guided Activity 10: Create a Project and Edit Project Settings

1. Start Camtasia.

2. Create a new project.

   ❑ from the **Home** area of the Home window, click **New Project**

   A new project is created immediately. While it would be easy to move forward with adding media assets to the timeline or canvas, it's a great idea to ensure the size of the project is set to the size you want first. If you resize a project after adding media to the canvas, you may need to resize the media assets to fit the new canvas size.

3. Change the size of the canvas.

   ❑ choose **File > Project Settings**

   ❑ from the **Canvas Dimensions** drop-down menu, choose **HD (1280x720)**

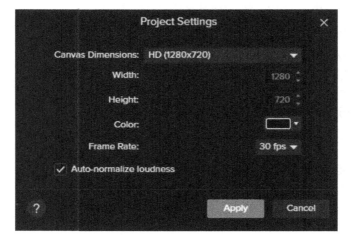

   ❑ click the **Apply** button

   As mentioned in the last module, most learner displays are wider than they are all tall. A rectangular project size of **1280x720** is very popular. The second most popular rectangular project size is FHD **1920x1080**.

Guided Activity 11: Import a Video into the Media Bin

1. Import a video into the Media Bin.

   ☐ from the list of tools at the left of the **Camtasia** window, click **Media** to display the **Media Bin**

   ☐ on the **Media Bin** panel, click **Import Media**

The Open dialog box appears. Any supported video file you can access from your computer can be imported into a Camtasia project using this dialog box.

Note: If you have not yet downloaded this book's support assets (also known as Data Files), turn to the **About This Book** section at the beginning of this book and work through the **Download and Extract the Data Files** activity on page viii.

   ☐ from the **Camtasia2023Data** folder, open the **Video_Files** folder

   ☐ open/import **CreateNewFolderVideo**

The video appears in the Media Bin.

Next you'll add the Media Bin video to the Timeline.

Guided Activity 12: Add Media to the Timeline

1. Add a Media Bin video to the Timeline.

   ☐ on the **Media Bin**, right-click the video you just imported

   ☐ choose **Add to Timeline at Playhead**

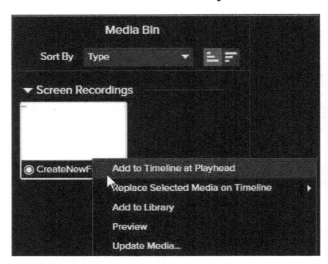

The video appears in two Camtasia locations: the Canvas and the Timeline. On the Timeline, the video is represented by a horizontal bar.

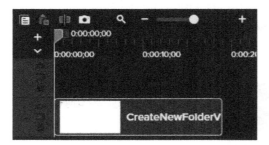

2. Preview a project on the Canvas.

   ☐ on the **Canvas**, click the **Play** button

As the video plays on the Canvas, notice that an object that moves along the Timeline. This object is known as the **Playhead**. You'll spend plenty of time working with the Playhead soon enough.

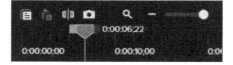

3. Save the project.

☐ choose **File > Save**

☐ open **Camtasia2023Data** > **Projects**

☐ name the Camtasia project **CreateNewFolder**

☐ from the bottom of the dialog box, ensure that **Create standalone project** is selected

As mentioned during the last module, the **Create standalone project** option bundles all of the imported Media Bin assets together with the project file. This feature ensures that anyone opening the project file with Camtasia 2023 or newer will have the assets needed to edit the project.

☐ click the **Save** button

PC users, you'll be alerted about opening the project file to make edits moving forward. You can click the **OK** button.

Depending upon your platform, saved projects get a slightly different file name extension. On the PC, files get a **tscproj** extension. Mac projects get a **cmproj** extension.

At the left, Camtasia for PC users and the tscproj extension. Projects on the Mac get a cmproj extension.

NOTES

Video Confidence Check

1. Ensure that the **CreateNewFolder** project is open.

2. On the **Timeline**, right-click the video you just added and choose **Delete**.

    The video is removed from the Timeline and, should the project be exported, the video will not be part of the final product. Even though the video has been removed from the Timeline, it remains a part of the project and is still in the Media Bin.

    Items in the Media Bin can always be previewed or added back onto the Timeline.

    Media Bin items are considered unused if they are not added to the Timeline at least one time.

3. Ensure the **Playhead** is positioned as far left of the Timeline as it will go.

4. Right-click the video in the Media Bin and choose **Add to Timeline at Playhead** to add the video back to the Timeline.

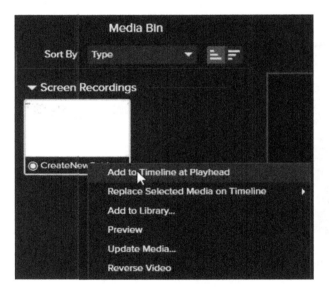

5. **Zoom closer** to the media in Track 1 by clicking the **Zoom timeline in** icon (located at the left of the Timeline).

    The ability to Zoom closer to Timeline objects will prove useful later when you need to split the audio or synchronize the video with other Timeline objects. You can always use the **Zoom timeline out** tool to move farther away from the Timeline or drag the slider (the circle between the plus and minus signs).

6. Save the project.

Adding Images

Few things enhance an eLearning lesson better than quality images. Camtasia supports many of the standard graphic formats, including bitmaps, GIFs, and JPEGs.

If you don't have access to photographs and other assets, I've had great success with BigStockPhoto.com and iStockPhoto.com. Both of these sites offer awesome collections of inexpensive, royalty-free assets.

You'll find free assets from TechSmith at https://library.techsmith.com. While many of the TechSmith Library assets are royalty-free, the use of some of their assets requires an annual subscription. There is also a Library located beneath the Media Bin that contains several free assets you can use in your projects. You'll explore the Library soon.

Guided Activity 13: Import Images to the Media Bin

1. Open an existing Camtasia project.

   ☐ choose **File > Open Project**

   ☐ from the **Camtasia2023Data > Projects** folder, open the **ImageMe** Camtasia project (from within the **ImageMe** folder)

   This project is identical to the one you were just working on. It has the CreateNewFolderVideo in the Media Bin and on the Timeline.

2. Import an image to the Media Bin.

   ☐ choose **File > Import > Media**

   ☐ from the **Camtasia2023Data** folder, open the **Image_Files** folder

   ☐ select **logo.png** and then click **Open** (PC) or **Import** (Mac)

   The logo image appears in the Media Bin.

3. Import another image.

   ☐ choose **File > Import > Media**

   ☐ from the **Image_Files** folder, open/import **mainart.jpg**

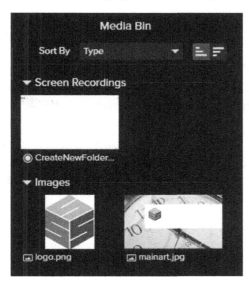

NOTES

Timeline Confidence Check

1. On the **Timeline**, drag the **CreateNewFolder** media to the **right** several seconds to leave space at the left for the **mainart** image. (You'll need at least 5 seconds of space to the left of the video media.)

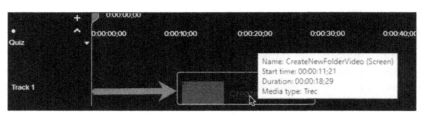

2. From the **Media Bin**, drag the **mainart** image to the beginning of Track 1 on the Timeline.

3. On the Timeline, there is likely a gap between the mainart object and the CreateNewFolder object. There are two ways you can remove the gap.

    Drag the **CreateNewFolder** object **left** until it bumps up against the mainart image (as shown in the first image below) *or* click the **Enable magnetic track** icon (as shown in the second image below)

4. On the **Canvas**, click the **Play** button to preview the project.

    On the Canvas, notice that the **mainart** image appears, disappears after a few seconds, and is then replaced by the video showing how to create a new folder.

    If you want Timeline objects to appear on the Canvas one after the other, you've just learned that it's as simple as dragging (or stretching) objects left or right on the Timeline to control when they appear and for how long. If you want multiple Timeline items on the Canvas at the same time, you'll need multiple Timeline tracks, something you'll learn about next.

5. Save your work.

Multi-Track Projects

You've added two assets to the Timeline (the video and the mainart image). Both objects appear on a single Timeline track called Track 1. You can easily add additional tracks to the Timeline. Once you have multiple tracks, you can precisely control when multiple objects appear on the Canvas and how items appear on the Canvas in relation to other Timeline media. For instance, you can add your corporate logo to a new track above the video track and create a watermark effect, perfect for corporate branding.

Guided Activity 14: Add a Track

1. Ensure that the **ImageMe** project is open.

2. Insert a new track.

   ☐ on the top left of the Timeline, click **Add a track**

   On the Timeline, notice that **Track 2** has been added just above Track 1. Because Track 2 is above Track 1 on the Timeline, anything you add to Track 2 appears to float (stacked) above anything on Track 1 when viewed on the Canvas.

3. Add an image to Track 2.

   ☐ if necessary, drag the **Playhead** to the **beginning** of the Timeline

   ☐ on the **Media Bin**, right-click the **logo** image and choose **Add to Timeline at Playhead**

NOTES

Only one object can be positioned on a track at a particular time on the Timeline. Because the Playhead is positioned at 0:00 time and there is an object on Track 1 at that time point, the logo is automatically added to the next available track (in this instance, the beginning of Track 2). If you hadn't manually added the second track prior to adding the image to the Timeline, the track would have been automatically added for you.

4. Change when the logo appears on the Timeline.

   ☐ on **Track 2** of the Timeline, position your mouse pointer in the **middle** of the **logo** object

   ☐ **drag** the logo object **right** until its **left edge** lines up with the left edge of the **CreateNewFolder** media on Track 1

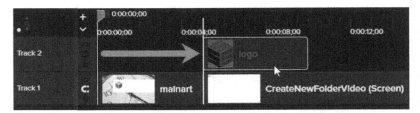

5. Position the Playhead and preview a portion of the video.

   ☐ on the **Timeline**, double-click the **CreateNewFolder** media

The Playhead, which indicates specific points in time and the current frame selected on the Timeline, should now be positioned just before the **CreateNewFolderVideo** object.

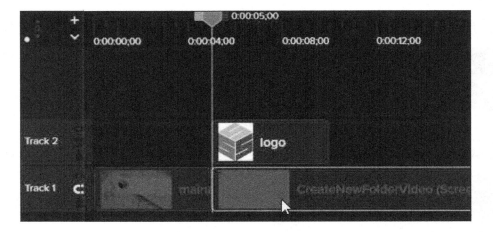

   ☐ on your keyboard, press [**spacebar**] to start previewing the video from the current Playhead position

On the Canvas, notice that the logo image appears above the video and then disappears after a few seconds (long before the video finishes).

6. Extend the play time for the logo.

   ❐ on the Timeline, use your mouse to **point** to the **right edge** of the logo object

   ❐ when your mouse pointer changes to a **double-headed arrow**, stretch the **right** edge of the logo object **right** until the logo's object bar aligns when the video ends (as shown in the image below)

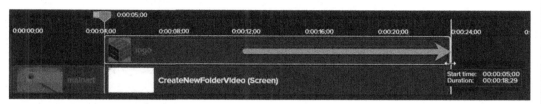

   Note: If you are too close or too far away from the Timeline, working with or aligning Timeline objects can be challenging.Consider zooming closer to the Timeline as appropriate prior to working with Timeline objects.

7. Preview the timing changes.

   ❐ on the Timeline, double-click the **CreateNewFolder** video object

   On the Timeline, the Playhead should once again appear just before the **CreateNewFolder** video on the Timeline.

   ❐ on your keyboard, press [**spacebar**] to Preview the project

   On the Canvas, notice that the logo image is visible for the duration of the video. However, the logo is too big, and it doesn't look good positioned in the middle of the Canvas. You will fix both issues next.

   ❐ on your keyboard, press [**spacebar**] again to stop the video preview

8. Save your work.

Guided Activity 15: Edit Media Properties

1. Ensure that the **ImageMe** project is open.

2. Display the Properties panel.

   ☐ on **Track 2,** right-click the **logo** and choose **Show Properties** (if you see **Hide Properties** in the menu instead of Show Properties, move to the next step)

   The Properties panel is located at the right side of the Camtasia window.

3. Use the Properties panel to make the logo smaller.

   ☐ near the top of the **Properties** panel, drag the **Scale** slider **left** to change the Scale to **50%** (if you find it difficult to get to exactly 50, type **50** into the Scale field at the right)

4. Lower the opacity of the logo.

   ☐ on the **Properties** panel, drag the **Opacity** slider **left** to change the Opacity to **40%** (again, if you find it difficult to get to exactly 40, type **40** into the field at the right)

5. Disable Canvas Snapping.

   ☐ choose **View > Enable Canvas Snapping** (ensure there is not a check mark next to the command)

6. Change the logo's Canvas position.

   ☐ on the Canvas, drag the logo near the **bottom right** of the video on the Canvas

   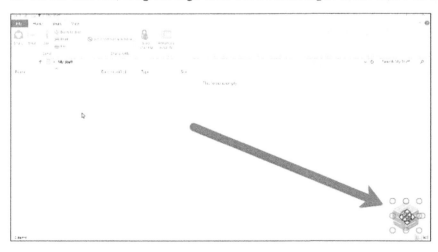

   By disabling Enable Canvas Snapping, you will be able to position Canvas objects more freely. If Enable Canvas Snapping is enabled, Canvas objects tend to snap to the edge of the Canvas.

7. Save your work.

Cursor Effects

Earlier in this module, you added a video to the project that demonstrates the process of creating a new folder on a computer (page 39). You've previewed that video several times during this module, so it's likely that you have already noticed that in the video the mouse, through the process of creating a new folder, moves from one part of the window to the next. As the cursor moves, there are no click sounds or visual effects to draw the learner's attention to the clicks. Because the video was created with the Camtasia Recorder, the cursor can be modified in the Editor by adding such enhancements as click effects and click sounds.

Guided Activity 16: Add Cursor Effects

1. Open an existing project.

   ☐ using Camtasia, choose **File > Open Project**

   ☐ from **Camtasia2023Data > Projects**, open the **MouseMe** folder and open the **MouseMe** project

2. Preview the video.

   ☐ on the **Timeline**, double-click the **CreateNewFolder** media object to move the Playhead to the beginning of the media

   ☐ on your keyboard, press [**spacebar**]

   As the video plays, notice the mouse cursor. The more cluttered the background, the harder the cursor may be for learners to see. During the steps that follow, you'll add a visual effect to make the cursor more noticeable onscreen.

3. Add a Highlight effect to the cursor in the video.

   ☐ on the **Timeline**, ensure that the **CreateNewFolderVideo** media is selected

   ☐ from the list of tools at the left, click **Cursor Effects**

   ☐ right-click the **Highlight** effect and choose **Add to Selected Media**

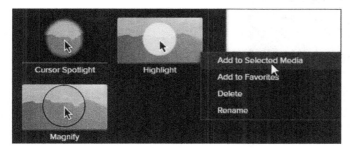

On the Timeline, the effect is added to the selected media. You can see the video effects (and delete them) via the Effects arrow beneath the video object on the Timeline.

NOTES

4. Preview the effect.

❑ on the **Timeline**, double-click the **CreateNewFolder** media to move the Playhead to the beginning of the video

❑ on your keyboard, press [**spacebar**]

The cursor now sports a nifty highlight effect. *How cool is that?*

❑ on your keyboard, press [**spacebar**] again to stop the Playhead and the preview

5. Change the Properties of the Cursor Effect.

❑ on the **Timeline**, right-click the **video media** and choose **Show Properties**

Note: If the menu item says **Hide Properties**, the Properties panel is already open at the right of the Camtasia window.

❑ at the top of the Properties panel, click the **Cursor Properties** icon

❑ on the **Properties** panel, **Highlight** area, **Color** section, select any color
❑ from the **Opacity** area, change the Opacity to **30%**
❑ from the **Size** area, drag the slider left to **30**

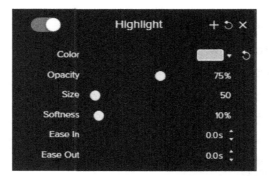

6. Preview the project.

The highlight's color, size, and opacity should reflect your changes.

Cursor Effects Confidence Check

1. On the Timeline, click **Show effects** just below the video media.

2. With the effects showing, right-click the **Highlight** effect and choose **Delete** (**Remove Effect** on the Mac) to delete it.

> **Note:** It's easy to accidentally delete media instead of a media effect. When deleting an effect, ensure that you right-click the effect, not the video itself.

3. Spend a few moments adding different **Cursor** effects to the video's cursor.

4. Spend a few moments adding **Left Click** effects to the video's cursor.

5. PC users, save your work.
   Mac users, save and close all open projects.

Modifying the Cursor Path and Size

You have already learned that you can add cursor effects to imported videos created with the Camtasia Recorder. However, the ability to add cursor effects is not limited to adding visual effects. If the size of your capture window is large and the recorded mouse pointer small, you can change the size of the cursor within Camtasia. And if, during the recording process, you moved the mouse pointer down and to the right when you really wanted to move up and to the left, you'll appreciate Camtasia's ability to simplify the path or create a new path.

Guided Activity 17: Smooth the Cursor Path

1. Create a new Camtasia project.

2. Change the Canvas size.

   ☐ choose **File > Project Settings**

   ☐ click the **Canvas Dimensions** drop-down menu

   ☐ choose **HD (1280x720)**

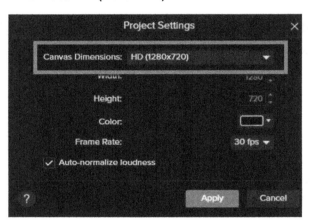

   ☐ click the **Apply** button

3. Import a video.

   ☐ choose **File > Import > Media**

   ☐ from **Camtasia2023Data > Video Files**, open **SmoothMyCursor**

4. Add the imported video to the timeline.

   ☐ on the **Media Bin**, right-click the video and choose **Add to Timeline at Playhead**

5. Use the Canvas to preview the video.

Notice both the size of the mouse pointer and the ragged path the cursor takes on its way to the Format menu. During the next few activities, you will learn how to smooth out the cursor path, modify the size of the cursor, and control both the cursor path and click speed. First, let's smooth out the cursor path and preview the results.

6. Save the project to the **Camtasia2023Data** folder with the name **Edited Cursor**.

7. Smooth the cursor path.

   ❒ from the list of tools at the left, click **Cursor Effects**

   ❒ on the **Timeline**, ensure that the **SmoothMyCursor** media is selected

   ❒ from the list of Cursor Effects, right-click **Cursor Smoothing** and choose **Apply to Selected Media**

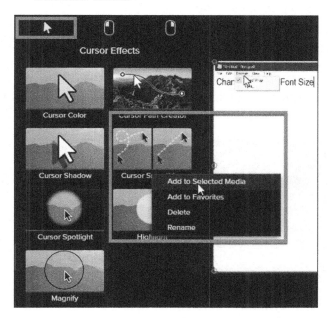

On the Timeline, notice that the Cursor Effect has been added to the media.

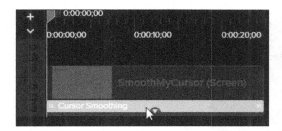

8. Use the Canvas to preview the video from the beginning.

NOTES

The path is smoother. However, the mouse sputters as it moves from point A to B to C.

9. Remove cursor pauses.

   ☐ on the **Properties** panel, **Cursor Smoothing** area, deselect **Detect Cursor Pauses** (remove the checkmark)

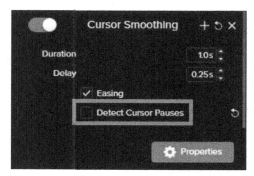

10. Use the Canvas to preview the video from the beginning.

    The cursor movement is better. However, the delay at the beginning of the video is not necessary. Let's trim away the first part of the video.

11. Trim a portion of the video.

    ☐ on the **Timeline**, observe the SmoothMyCursor media

    Each of the icons on the media represent potential cursor movement. Because of the smoothing effect, the first part of the video is not needed.

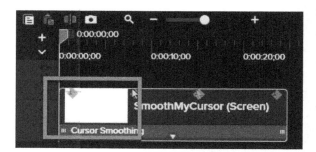

    ☐ on the **Timeline**, position the **Playhead** at the **beginning** of the video media

    ☐ on the **Timeline**, drag the **red** icon next to the **Playhead** to the **right** until just before the second mouse movement icon

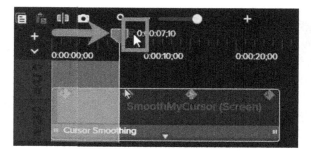

❏ on the **Timeline**, click the **cut** icon ✂

12. Use the Canvas to preview the video from the beginning.

Now that you've trimmed away the first part of the video, the cursor moves sooner but its Canvas position has changed... now the cursor is positioned over the Format menu right away. If you want to have full control over the cursor, you need to control the cursor path. Let's remove the media from the Timeline and learn how to edit the cursor path.

13. Remove the media from the Timeline.

❏ on the **Timeline**, right-click the **SmoothMyCursor** media and choose **Delete**

14. Add the media back to the Timeline.

❏ on the **Timeline**, position the Playhead back at the beginning

❏ on the **Media Bin**, right-click the imported video and choose **Add to Timeline at Playhead**

15. Save your work and keep the project open for the next activity.

Guided Activity 18: Edit the Cursor Path

1. Ensure that the **Edited Cursor** project you created during the previous activity is still open.

2. Ensure that the **SmoothMyCursor** media is on the Timeline.

3. Use the Canvas to preview the video.

   Notice that the cursor path is not very smooth. You have already learned that you can quickly smooth out the cursor path. However, for complete control over the cursor, you need to edit its path.

4. Edit the cursor path.

   ☐ on the **Timeline**, select the video media

   ☐ on the **Properties** panel, click the **Cursor Properties** icon

   ☐ on the **Properties** panel, click the **Edit Cursor Path** button

   The Edit Cursor Path options open.

   ☐ from the **Option** drop-down menu, choose **Simplify Existing Path** (if necessary)

   ☐ click the **Continue** button

5. Move the Playhead to see the cursor points.

   ☐ on the **Timeline**, drag the **Playhead** left and then right a few times

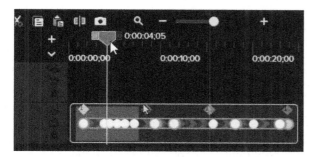

   On the Canvas, you can see editable cursor points.

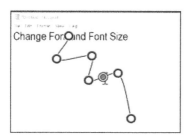

6. Delete a cursor point.

   ☐ on the **Timeline**, move the Playhead to **3;28**

   ☐ on the **Canvas**, select the cursor point shown in the box below

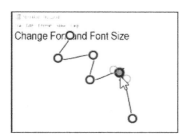

   ☐ **right-click** the cursor point and choose **Delete Cursor Point**

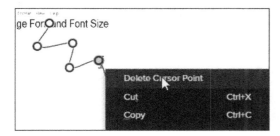

---

7. Move a cursor point.

☐ on the **Canvas**, select the cursor point shown in the box below

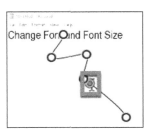

☐ **drag** the cursor down and to the right until it is centered between the cursor points

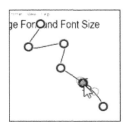

Cursor Paths Confidence Check

1. Continue to edit the mouse path at the beginning of the video similar to the path shown in the image below.

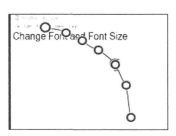

2. Preview the video from the beginning.

   Notice that the edited path is no longer ragged like it was before. However, there is a delay between each of the cursor points and the cursor movement is not very smooth. There are two ways to address the delays. You can add cursor points or use the Timeline to close up the delay between points.

3. On the Canvas, right-click between two points and choose **Add Cursor Point**.

4. Continue adding a few more cursor points along the cursor path.

5. Preview the video and notice that the cursor path is now even smoother.

6. On the Timeline, zoom closer to the video media.

    The cursor points are shown as the white dots along the Timeline. The gaps between the cursor points represent the delays.

7. Drag some of the highlighted cursor point left to remove gaps between the points.

8. Preview the video and notice that the speed of the mouse motion is better and better.

9. Spend a few moments removing the delay between additional cursor points.

10. When satisfied with the path and the timing, click the **Finish Editing** button on the Properties panel.

    Note: You can restore the original cursor path by clicking the **Restore Path** button.

NOTES

Guided Activity 19: Change the Cursor Appearance and Size

1. Ensure that the Edited Cursor project you created during the previous activity is still open.

2. Change the appearance of the cursor.

   ☐ on the **Timeline**, select the video media

   ☐ on the **Properties** panel, click the **Cursor Properties** icon

   ☐ from the **Cursor** area, click the drop-down menu

   ☐ from the drop-down menu beneath that, choose **Windows Cursors** or **Mac cursors**

   ☐ select any cursor you like

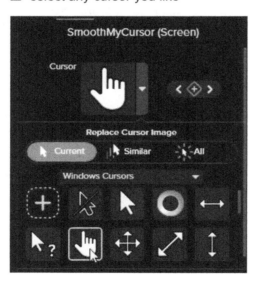

3. Change the size of the cursor.

   ☐ on the Properties panel, drag the **Scale** slider **left** or **right** to resize the cursor as you see fit

4. Preview the video to see the results.

5. Save the project. (Mac users, close the project.)

iCONLOGiC

"Skills and Drills" Learning

Module 4: Groups, Annotations, and Animation

In This Module You Will Learn About:

And You Will Learn To:

Groups

Changing the timing for media objects on the Timeline is easy—just drag and drop objects left or right along the Timeline, or drag objects up or down on the Timeline to change tracks. However, moving Timeline objects can negatively impact how Timeline objects are synchronized with other Timeline objects on different tracks. For instance, let's say that you have an image on track 1 positioned perfectly on the Timeline so that it appears on the Canvas along with a video on track 2. If you reposition the image in track 1 but forget to also reposition the track 2 video, the timing between the two media objects is no longer synchronized. Because object relationships across multiple tracks can be complex, you'll appreciate Camtasia's ability to group objects. Rather than moving an individual Timeline object, you can group objects, even across multiple tracks, and move multiple Timeline objects at once.

Guided Activity 20: Create a Group

1. Using Camtasia, open the **AnnotateMe** project from **Camtasia2023Data > Projects**.

2. Move a Timeline object.

   ☐ on the **Timeline**, drag the **logo** media to the **right** by a few seconds

   After moving the logo, notice that the CreateNewFolderVideo object does not move. Given that these two objects should appear onscreen together, it would be better to group them prior to moving either one of them.

3. Undo the last step.

   ☐ choose **Edit > Undo**

   The logo should now be back in its original Timeline position.

4. Create a group.

   ☐ on the **Timeline**, select the **CreateNewFolderVideo** media in Track **1**

   ☐ press [**shift**] and select the **logo** in Track **2** (then release [**shift**])

   Both the video and the logo should now be selected.

   ☐ choose **Edit > Group**

   The selected independent objects are now grouped. The logo, which was in Track 2, has been moved into the new group on Track 1

Note: To Ungroup a group, right-click a group and choose **Ungroup**.

If you double-click a group, it opens so that objects within the group can be edited or replaced. To close an open group, click the close group icon on the Timeline.

5. Rename a group.

   ❏ on the **Timeline**, right-click the group in Track **1** and choose **Rename Group**

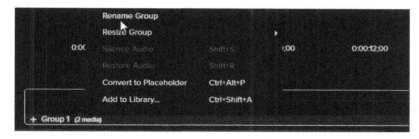

The group's default name, Group 1, is selected.

   ❏ change the group's name to **Creating Folders** and press [**enter**]

6. Move Timeline objects as a group.

   ❏ on the **Timeline**, position the Playhead at the 30 second mark

   ❏ on the **Timeline**, drag the **Creating Folders** group **right** until its left edge lines up with the **30 second** mark on the **Timeline**

Both objects in the group move, leaving a sizable gap between the mainart object and the Creating Folders group. You'll be adding media within the gap soon.

7. Remove an empty track.

   ❏ at the left of the Timeline, right-click the words **Track 2** and choose **Remove All Empty Tracks**

Note: Empty tracks do no harm, and it is never a requirement to remove them.

Annotations

Annotations are typically used to add text/context to your video. There are several types of Annotations, including **Callouts** (shapes that can contain text), Arrows, Lines, Shapes, Motions, and Keystrokes. In the Demo project you opened at the beginning of this book, there are several callouts synchronized with the voiceover narration. One of the callouts from that project is shown in the image below (the callout contains the words **CREATE** and **FOLDERS**). During the activities that follow, you will add and then format a few callouts.

Guided Activity 21: Add a Callout

1. Ensure that the **AnnotateMe** project is open.

2. Insert a callout.

   ☐ on the **Timeline**, double-click the **mainart** image to move the Playhead to the **far left** of the Timeline

   ☐ from the list of tools at the left, click **Annotations**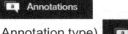

   ☐ on the **Annotations** panel, click **Callouts** (the first Annotation type)

   ☐ from the **Style** drop-down menu, choose **Basic**

   ☐ right-click the **white rectangle with the black text** and choose **Add to Timeline at Playhead**

Because the Playhead was positioned at 00:00 on the **Timeline**, and there was media already on Track 1 at that moment in time, a new track is automatically added to accommodate the new caption.

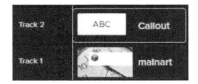

3. Remove a callout's border.

☐ ensure that the new annotation is selected

☐ at the top of the **Properties** panel, click the **Annotation Properties** icon

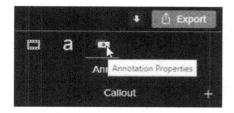

☐ on the callout **Properties** panel, change the **Thickness** to **0** (you can either type a **0** into the text field or drag the slider as far **left** as it will go)

4. Format the callout's text.

☐ with the annotation still selected, at the top of the **Properties** panel, click **Text Properties**

☐ change the Font to **Verdana (Regular)**

☐ change the Color to **Black**

☐ change the Size to **80**

☐ change the Alignment to **Left**

☐ deselect **Auto-resize Text**

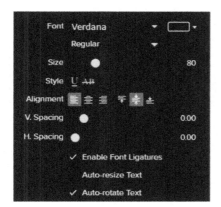

Auto-resize Text, if selected, will make your text smaller should you type more text into the text box than will fit. By deselecting Auto-resize text, you're ensuring that the font size used in this Annotation will always be 80 points.

NOTES

5. Add the callout text.

❏ replace the existing text in the callout with the words **CREATE FOLDERS**

❏ resize and position the callout similar to the image below

6. Save your work.

Themes

Most companies require a consistent use of annotation fonts and colors from one project to another. Similar to Object Styles in other development tools and Word processors you've likely used, Themes can contain several formatting options. Once you've created and set up a Theme, you can quickly apply it to selected Timeline objects and quickly gain a measure of formatting consistency.

Guided Activity 22: Apply and Create Themes

1. Ensure that the **AnnotateMe** project is open.

2. Add a second callout to the Timeline.

   ❑ from the **Annotations** tools, click **Callouts**

   ❑ from the **Style** drop-down menu, choose **Basic**

   ❑ on the **Timeline**, double-click the **mainart** image to move the Playhead to the **far left** of the Timeline

   ❑ right-click the **white rectangle with the black text** and choose **Add to Timeline at Playhead**

   The new callout is using formatting defaults and does not match the appearance of your first callout.

3. Apply Themes to an object.

   ❑ with the newest callout selected on the Canvas, click either the **Text Properties** icon or **Annotation Properties** icon on the **Properties** panel

   ❑ from the **Theme** drop-down menu, choose **Default**

   The font formatting and background color of the selected callout change to reflect the properties of the Default Theme.

4. Create a new Theme.

   ❑ with the newest callout selected, click the **Theme** drop-down menu and choose **Manage Themes**

The first time you select Manage Themes, you will see an alert. The alert, which gives a high-level overview of a theme, will not appear a second time.

❑ click the **OK** button

The **Theme Manager** opens.

❑ click the **Create New Theme** icon (the **plus sign**)

The New Theme dialog box opens.

❑ name the new Theme **SuperSim Theme**

❑ click the **OK** button

The SuperSim theme opens and is ready for editing.

5. Set a Theme's Font.

   ☐ from within the **Theme Manager**, and with the **SuperSim Theme** selected, click the **Fonts** tab

   ☐ change **Font 1** to **Verdana**

6. Set a Theme's Colors.

   ☐ from within the **Theme Manager**, and with the **SuperSim Theme** selected, click the **Colors** tab

   ☐ change the **Foreground** color to **Black** (this controls the color of the text in the callout)

   ☐ change the **Background1** color to **White**

   ☐ change the **Annotation Background** to **Background1**

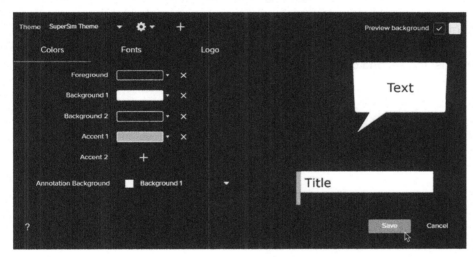

   ☐ click the **Save** button

7. Apply Themes to multiple callouts.

   ☐ select both of the callouts you've added to the Timeline so far (selecting one and [**shift**]-**clicking** the second one works great)

   ☐ from the **Themes** drop-down menu on the **Properties** panel, choose **Default**

   Both callouts take on the attributes of the Default Theme.

   ☐ with both callouts still selected, click the **Themes** drop-down menu and choose **SuperSim Theme**

NOTES

Both annotations take on the attributes of the SuperSim Theme.

If you've used styles in other programs, then the behavior of a Theme will be familiar to you. Unfortunately, the formatting power of Camtasia Themes is limited. You cannot control many of an object's Properties with a Theme, such as border thickness, color, or drop shadows). Moreover, if you update a Theme, objects using the Theme do not automatically receive the changes. You need to manually reselect objects and reapply the Theme. I'm hopeful that as Camtasia continues to be updated by TechSmith, more and more formatting power will be added to the Themes feature.

8. Delete just the second callout you added.

Guided Activity 23: Apply Image Color to Callout Text

1. Ensure that the **AnnotateMe** project is open.

2. Pick up color from an image and apply it to selected text.

   ☐ on the **Canvas**, double-click the callout and highlight the word **CREATE**.

   ☐ at the top of the **Properties** panel, click the **Text Properties** icon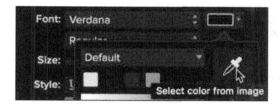

   ☐ from the **font color** drop-down menu, select the **eyedropper** icon

   ☐ using the **eyedropper**, click the green "**S**" on the logo

   The logo color you clicked with the **eyedropper** tool is applied to the highlighted text in the callout.

   CREATE FOLDERS

3. Save your work.

Callouts Confidence Check

1. Click in front of the word **FOLDERS** and press [**enter**].

2. Press [spacebar] a few times to indent the word **FOLDERS**.

3. On the **Timeline**, right-click the callout annotation and **Copy** it to the clipboard.

4. On the **Timeline**, position the **Playhead** just to the **right** of the callout.

5. PC users, right-click the existing callout and choose **Paste**.
   Mac users, right-click just to the right of the callout and choose **Paste Media at Playhead**

6. Drag the newest callout so it is positioned just after the first callout in Track 2.

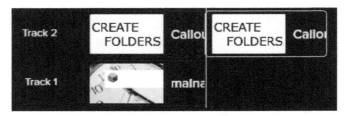

7. Double-click the new callout and change the word **CREATE** to **RENAME**.

RENAME
FOLDERS

8. On the **Timeline**, position the Playhead just to the right of the second callout.

9. PC users, right-click the existing callout and choose **Paste**.
   Mac users, right-click just to the right of the callout and choose **Paste Media at Playhead**

10. Drag the newest callout so it is positioned just after the second callout in Track 2.

11. Drag the new callout up against the second callout.

12. Double-click the new callout and change the word **CREATE** to **DELETE**.

13. Change the word **FOLDERS** to **RESTORE**.

14. Save your work.

15. Create a **new** Camtasia project.

16. Spend a few moments adding some of the other Annotations to the project. (There is no need to save the new project so play as much as you'd like.)

As you add the Annotations, notice the formatting options available to you on the Properties panel. You'll find that the options vary depending upon the type of Annotation you're working with.

17. Select any annotation and notice that there is a star in the upper right.

18. Click the star icon to turn it yellow and add the object as a **Favorite**.

19. From the tools at the left, click **Favorites** to see the shape that you've just added. From this point you can easily add the object to your Timeline or Canvas. (You can remove a Favorite by right-clicking and choosing **Remove Favorite**.)

    Note: Favorites added to one project will be available to all projects.

20. Mac users, you can close the project (there is no need to save when prompted). PC users, you'll be prompted to save the project when opening the next one. There is no need to save when prompted.

Behaviors

Behaviors are animations that are typically used to add some visual appeal to your project. Behaviors can be attached to images, video clips, and several types of Annotations. A Behavior can be added to a single object or stacked together with other Behaviors to create unique effects.

Guided Activity 24: Add a Behavior to a Callout

1. Using Camtasia, open the **BehaveMe** project from **Camtasia2023Data > Projects**.

   This project has several callouts that have been added to Tracks 2 and 3. In particular, notice the three ampersands (**&**) added to Track 2 at **10;05**, **15;18**, and **20;18**.

   The stacking order of assets on the Timeline is important. Notice that each ampersand is **behind** the callouts you added earlier. The stacking effect was easily attained by placing the ampersand in a lower Timeline track.

   In the image above, the **DELETE RESTORE** callout is in Track 3; the ampersand is in Track 2. Objects in higher tracks are positioned above objects in lower tracks.

   In the next step, you'll be adding a Behavior to the ampersands.

2. Add a Behavior to a callout.

   ☐ on Track 2, double-click the first **ampersand** positioned at **10;05** on the **Timeline** to highlight object on both the Timeline and on the Canvas

   ☐ from the list of tools at the left, click **Behaviors**

   ☐ right-click **Jump And Fall** and choose **Add to Selected Media**

The Jump and Fall effect is added to the callout and appears below the Timeline object in the Effects area. Any effect can be removed from an object by showing the effects, right-clicking an effect, and then choosing **Delete** (PC) or **Remove Effect** (Mac).

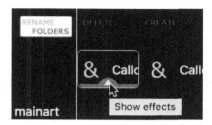

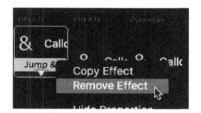

3. Preview the effect.

   ❏ on the **Timeline**, move the **Playhead** just to the left of the **ampersand** you just altered

   ❏ press [**spacebar**] on your keyboard **or** click the **Play** button on the Canvas

   When the Playhead gets to **DELETE RESTORE** callout, the ampersand drops in from the top of the Canvas, bounces a few times, and then drops off the bottom of the Canvas. Next you'll delay the appearance of the ampersand to enhance the effect.

4. Use the Timeline to delay the appearance of an object on the Canvas.

   ❏ on the **Timeline**, drag the **left edge** of the **ampersand** callout **right** a few seconds

5. Preview the timing change.

   ❏ on the **Timeline**, move the **Playhead** just to the left of the **RENAME FOLDERS** callout (the second callout on Track 2)

   ❏ press [**spacebar**] on your keyboard **or** click the **Play** button on the Canvas

   A few seconds after the **DELETE RESTORE** callout appears on the Canvas, the animated ampersand appears and does its thing.

6. Modify the Properties of a Behavior.

   ❏ on Track 2, double-click the **ampersand** you've been working with (the first ampersand) to highlight it on the Canvas

   Currently, the ampersand drops in from the top of the Canvas. Let's see what other tricks you can make the callout perform.

NOTES

☐ on the **Properties** panel, select **Behavior Properties**

The Jump & Fall effect has three tabs: **In**, **During**, and **Out**. The **In** tab allows you to control what the Effect does when the object first makes an appearance on the Canvas. The **During** tab controls what the object does while it's on the Canvas. The **Out** tab lets you control what the effect does when the object leaves the Canvas.

☐ from the **Jump & Fall** Properties area, select the **In** tab

☐ from the **Style** drop-down menu, choose **Hinge**

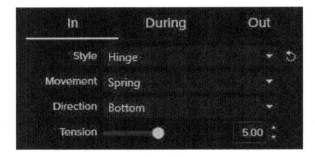

Behaviors Confidence Check

1. With the Playhead positioned just to the left of the **ampersand** you just altered, preview the effect on the Canvas.

   The ampersand should swing up from the bottom of the Canvas.

2. Spend a few moments playing with the **In**, **During**, and **Out** settings available on the **Properties** panel.

3. Add a Behavior to the remaining two ampersands (the ampersands are positioned on the **Timeline** at **15;18**, and **20;18**).

4. Preview the effects and adjust the timing of the ampersand callouts as you see fit.

5. Adjust the **In**, **During**, and **Out** properties of the effects as you see fit.

6. Select and then group mainart image and the callouts (name the group **Introduction to folders**).

7. Save your work. (Mac users, close the project.)

Transitions

You can use Transitions to add a smooth, professional visual break between clips in a project. There are several Transition types available on the Transitions panel, including Arrow Slice, Bar Wipe, Blob, Blur, Cube, and more.

Guided Activity 25: Add a Transition to a Group

1. Using Camtasia, open the **TransitionMe** project from **Camtasia2023Data** > **Projects**.

2. Add a Transition to selected media.

   ☐ from the tools at the left, click **Transitions**

   ☐ on the **Timeline**, select the **Get Ready** group

   ☐ on the **Transitions** panel, right-click the **Blob** transition and choose **Add to Selected Media**

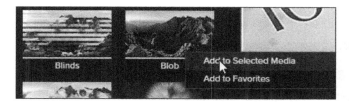

On the Timeline, the Blob transition has been added to the beginning of the selected group, and it's been added to the beginning of the next group. You can tell that a transition has been added via the green rectangles. The transition was added to the second group (even though you didn't select that group) because, by default, transitions are added to the beginning and end of a selected group and to the beginning of the next group that it is touching.

3. Save your work.

NOTES

NOTES

Guided Activity 26: Modify Transition Timing

1. Ensure that the **TransitionMe** project is open.

2. Preview the project from the beginning.

   As the video plays on the Canvas, the Blob transition appears at the beginning and end of the first clip and again at the beginning of the second clip. It's a cool effect, but you'd like to speed it up a bit.

3. Modify Transition Timing.

   ☐ on the **Timeline**, drag the **right edge** of the first green transition icon a bit to the **left**

   ☐ drag the **left** edge second green transition a bit to the **right**

4. Preview the project from the beginning.

   The timing for each transition should be a bit faster than before.

Transitions Confidence Check

1. Working in the **TransitionMe** project, add any transition(s) you like to each of the groups.

2. Preview the project to see the transitions.

3. Edit the speed of the transitions as you see fit.

4. Save your work.

Custom Animation

By now, you've seen that Camtasia is a powerhouse when it comes to recording screen actions, is flexible when it comes to adding media, and is loaded with built-in animations you can add to Timeline objects including, but not limited to, transitions and behaviors.

Let's crank things up a notch and create a custom animation. You're about to launch a rocket into the sky, fly around a bit, and then land the rocket back where it started. Move over, SpaceX!

Guided Activity 27: Create an Animation

1. Using Camtasia, open the **LaunchMeLandMe** project from **Camtasia2022Data > Projects**.

2. Add a Custom Animation to Timeline media.

   ☐ on Track **3** of the **Timeline**, select the **Rocket** media

   ☐ from the list of tools at the left, select **Animations**

   Note: PC users, there are two tabs grouped with Animations. Select the second tab, **Animations**.

   ☐ drag the **Custom** animation onto the **Rocket** media on the **Timeline** (don't drag the animation to the Canvas but to the Timeline media)

   An arrow appears on the Timeline. The arrow represents the animation. The left edge of the arrow, the smaller circle, represents what happens when the animation begins. The right edge, the larger circle, represents what happens when the animation ends.

   ☐ drag the animation arrow **left** or **right** until its left edge is aligned at **1;00**

   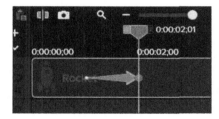

   ☐ on the animation arrow, select the larger circle and, on the **Canvas**, drag the rocket up into the sky

3. Drag the Playhead to the beginning of the Timeline and then preview the video.

    The rocket lifts off from the launch pad.

4. Add another Custom animation.

    ☐ drag a second Custom animation onto the Timeline and position it just to the **right** of the first one

    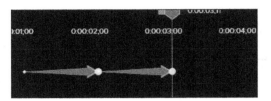

    ☐ on the **Timeline**, select the larger circle of the newest animation arrow

    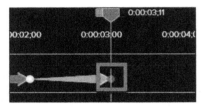

    ☐ on the **Canvas**, select the **Rotate** icon and rotate the rocket so that it is on its side

5. Drag the Playhead to the beginning of the Timeline and then preview the video.

    Notice that the rocket lifts off from the landing and then rotates to face right.

6. Add another Custom animation.

    ☐ drag a third **Custom** animation onto the Timeline and position it just to the right of the second one

☐ on the **Timeline**, select the larger circle on the newest animation

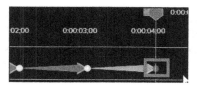

☐ on the **Canvas**, drag the rocket to the **right** side of the screen

7. Drag the Playhead to the beginning of the Timeline and then preview the video.

This time, the rocket lifts off from the landing, rotates, and then flies across the screen.

Animation Confidence Check

Your mission now is to return the rocket safely to the landing pad.

1. Add more custom animations to the Timeline.

☐ one animation should turn the rocket back up into the sky

☐ one animation should turn the rocket back toward the left side of the screen

☐ one animation should rotate the rocket into the landing position

☐ one final animation should allow the rocket to land.

2. Preview the animation.

3. Save the project.

NOTES

Corner Pin Mode

Using Corner Pin Mode, you can integrate media on the Canvas and create the illusion that the assets were created to work together. In the activity that follows, you'll add two assets to the Canvas: an image of a person using a tablet and a video demonstration. The two assets were never intended to be shown onscreen together because the angles in the image do not match the angles in the video. Using Corner Pin Mode, you will change the angles of the video so it works remarkably well with the image.

Guided Activity 28: Use Corner Pin Mode

1. Create a new Camtasia project.

2. Add media to the Media Bin and the Timeline.

   ☐ choose **File > Import > Media**

   ☐ from **Camtasia2023Data > Image_Files**, open **tablet.jpg**

   ☐ on the **Media Bin**, right-click the tablet image and choose **Add to Timeline at Playhead**

   ☐ choose **File > Import > Media**

   ☐ from **Camtasia2023Data > Video_Files**, open **CreateNewFolderVideo.trec**

   ☐ on the **Media Bin**, right-click the video and choose **Add to Timeline at Playhead**

3. Extend the playtime of the image.

   ☐ on the **Timeline**, stretch the tablet media in Track 1 until its playtime is equal to the playtime of the video in Track 2

4. Use the Corner Pin feature to fit the video within the tablet image.

   ☐ on the **Canvas**, resize the **video** media to approximately one-third of its current size (about the size of the tablet in the background image)

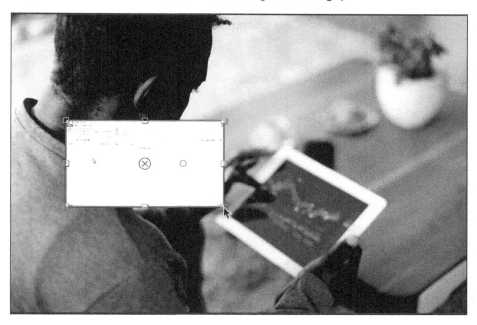

   ☐ with the video media selected, click the **Corner Pin Mode** icon (the icon is above the Canvas)

   ☐ on the **Canvas**, drag the video media over the image of the tablet in the background (if the video is a bit too large or too small, you can resize it later)

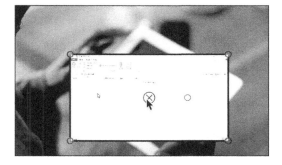

   ☐ on the **Canvas**, **drag** the **top left corner** of the video media until it matches the top left corner of the screen within the tablet image

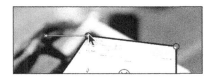

Corner Pin Mode Confidence Check

1. Choose **View > Enable Canvas Snapping** to **disable** the feature. (Remove the checkmark from beside the menu item.)

2. Continue dragging the corners of the video media to match the shape of the tablet screen in the background image.

   With Canvas Snapping disabled, you are able to more precisely match the corners of the video media with the background image.

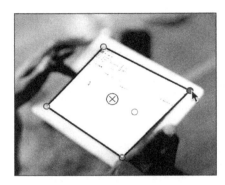

   Note: If you need to resize the video, return to **Edit** mode. If you need to make more edits to the video skew, return to Corner Pin Mode.

3. Preview the results.

   How cool is it be able to seamlessly integrate an image with a video?

4. Save the project to the **Camtasia2023Data > Projects** folder as **MyCornerPinMode**.

Module 5: Audio

In This Module You Will Learn About:

And You Will Learn To:

Audio Media

You can import four types of audio media into a Camtasia project: WAV, MP3, WMA, and M4A. The most common audio formats among the four types are WAV and MP3.

WAV (WAVE): WAV files are one of the original digital audio standards. Although high in quality, WAV files can be very large. Typical WAV audio files can easily take up to several megabytes of storage per minute of playing time. If your learner has a slow Internet connection, the download time for large files is unacceptable. **MP3** (MPEG Audio Layer III): Developed in Germany by the Fraunhofer Institute, MP3 files are compressed digital audio files. File sizes in this format are typically 90 percent smaller than WAV files.

You will find a few sound files in the Camtasia Library, and there are additional resources among the TechSmith Camtasia audio assets at **https://library.techsmith.com/camtasia** via a paid subscription. According to TechSmith, you can use their media assets in a Camtasia project royalty-free. When something from a trusted source is labeled royalty-free, it means you can confidently use those assets without the need to pay additional fees to the copyright holder. However, before using assets obtained from any other source, you should ensure you have documented permission to use those assets for your intended purpose.

Guided Activity 29: Add Music From the Library

1. Using Camtasia, open the **AudioMe** project from **Camtasia2023Data > Projects**.

2. Add background music to the project from the Library.

   ☐ on the **Timeline**, ensure the **Playhead** is positioned at the **beginning**

   ☐ from the list of tools at the left, click **Library**

   ☐ from the **Library** drop-down menu, ensure that **Camtasia 2023** is selected

   ☐ on the **Library**, open the **Audio** folder

   ☐ right-click any of the audio files and choose **Add to Timeline at Playhead**

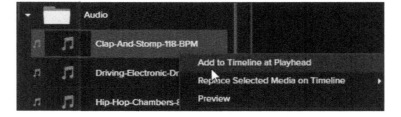

   The audio media appears on the Timeline in Track 2.

Library Audio Confidence Check

1. Preview the project to hear the audio.

2. On the **Timeline**, select and delete the audio media you just added.

3. On the **Media Bin**, notice that although you've removed the music from the Timeline, a copy of the unused media asset is retained in the Bin.

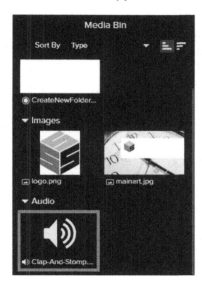

4. From the **Library**, add a different audio file to the Timeline.

5. Preview the project to hear the music track.

6. on the **Timeline**, select and delete the music track.

7. On the **Media Bin,** notice that the newest music is also listed even though it is no longer being used on the Timeline (along with the first music track you added).

8. Right-click the Media Bin and choose **Delete Unused Media**.

Note: Deleting unused media isn't a requirement but does keep the Media Bin clutter-free and will reduce the size of your project folder.

9. Save your work.

Guided Activity 30: Import Music

1. Ensure that the **AudioMe** project is open.

2. Import an audio file to the Media Bin.

   ☐ choose **File > Import > Media**

   ☐ navigate to **Camtasia2023Data > Audio_Files**

   ☐ from the **Audio_Files** folder, open/import **2Step1.mp3**

   The imported music track appears in the Media Bin.

3. Add the imported audio to the Timeline.

   ☐ ensure the **Playhead** is positioned at the **beginning** of the **Timeline**

   ☐ on the **Media Bin**, right-click **2Step1.mp3** and choose **Add to Timeline at Playhead**

4. Preview the project to hear the music track you just added to the Timeline.

   If you listen to the music until the end, you'll notice that the audio fades out nicely. However, if you preview the beginning of the project, you'll notice that the music starts just a bit too abruptly. You will take care of that next when you learn how to fade music.

Guided Activity 31: Fade Audio

1. Ensure that the **AudioMe** project is open.

2. Fade audio in.

   ☐ on the **Timeline**, select the **2Step1** music track on **Track 2**

   ☐ from the tools at the left, click **Audio Effects**

   ☐ from the **Audio Effects** panel, right-click **Fade In** and choose **Add to Selected Media**

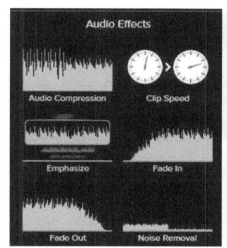 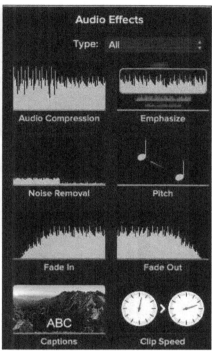

Shown above, the Audio Effects for Camtasia 2023 for Windows; at the right, the Mac version of Camtasia 2023.

Notice that a "ramp" has been added to the left of the waveform.

The ramp begins at the bottom of the waveform and then gets taller until the audio hits a consistent level. You can manually drag the green line to control how the audio fades in, but you'll probably be happy with the level established automatically by Camtasia.

3. Preview the beginning of the project to hear the audio fade-in effect.

4. If you'd like the fade effect to last a bit longer, drag the green circle on the audio media **right** to extend the fade timing.

NOTES

Fading Confidence Check

1. Delete the background music from the Timeline.

2. Using the Library, add any Music Track to the Timeline.

   The music that you just added to the Timeline plays far longer than your other Timeline assets.

3. Drag the **right side** of the background music **left** until the end of the music lines up with the assets in the last group on the **Timeline**.

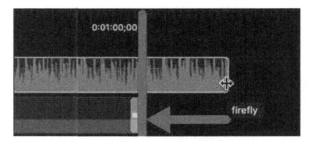

4. Use the **Audio Effects** to add **Fade In** and/or **Fade Out** effects to the music on the **Timeline** as you see fit.

5. Preview the project to hear the fade effects.

6. Save your work. (Mac users: You can close the project.)

Voice Narration

Camtasia allows you to record your voice and sound effects and add them to the Timeline. If you plan to record audio, consider the following:

Voiceover Scripts: There is a voiceover script called **CreatingFoldersVoiceoverScript** in **Camtasia2023Data > Other Assets**. You'll be opening that script soon. It's a good idea to write and then rehearse the voiceover script before recording the audio in Camtasia. Rehearsals are the perfect opportunity to find any areas of the script that are going to cause you problems while recording (trouble pronouncing words, for example, or wordiness).

Location, Location, Location: You might be surprised by how much noise there is in an average office or home. Is there a nearby faucet dripping? Is the overhead fan making noise? Is your neighbor or family member coughing or sneezing? It's possible you're creating your eLearning at home where you're sure it's quieter. But is the dog barking? Are the kids playing just outside your door? While you have become adept at tuning out everyday sounds, your microphone hears— and records—everything. Before using your office or cubicle as a recording studio, stop and listen to what's happening around you, and try to get your surroundings as quiet as possible.

Microphones vs. Headsets: A microphone is what you'll use to record your audio. It can be positioned on your desk, on a stand, suspended from the ceiling, or attached to your clothing. Typical headsets combine a microphone, typically a boom that can be adjusted up and down and further or closer to your mouth, and a listening device. As the name implies, a headset is usually positioned on your head. You can use either a microphone or a headset when you record audio. If you'd like to see and hear a side-by-side comparison of several recording devices, **Rick Zanotti** is an excellent resource. Visit **youtube.com** and search for "**eLearnChat Microphones for eLearning**" for an entire video series Rick created that covers everything from Sennheiser to Shure to Neumann to Blue Bird.

Microphone Placement: The microphone should be positioned approximately six inches from your mouth to reduce the chance that nearby sounds will be recorded. Ideally, you should position the microphone above your nose and pointed down at your mouth. Also, if you position the microphone just to the side of your mouth, you can soften the sound of the letters S and P.

Microphone Technique: It's a good idea to keep a glass of water close and, just before recording, take a drink. To eliminate breathing and lip-smack sounds, turn away from the microphone, take a deep breath, exhale, take another deep breath, open your mouth, turn back toward the microphone, and start speaking. Speak slowly. When recording for the first time, many people race through the content. *Take your time.*

Monitor Your Audio Level As You Record: When recording your audio, you will see an Input Level meter on Camtasia's Voice Narration panel indicating how well the recording process is going. When the meter is green to yellow, you're fine. However, when the meter is orange to red, you are being warned that you are too close to the microphone or that you are speaking too loudly.

Guided Activity 32: Record Voice Narration

1. Using a word processor, open **CreatingFoldersVoiceoverScript** from **Camtasia2023Data > Other_Assets**.

   Let's pretend for a moment that you've been hired to serve as the voiceover talent for the eLearning project. It's quite possible you'd get a script similar to the file you've just opened.

   > **Audio File 1:**
   > Welcome to Super Simplistic Solutions learning series.
   > This is lesson one: Creating New Folders.
   >
   > **Audio File 2:**
   > This lesson is going to teach you how to create a new folder on your computer, how to rename it, and how to both delete and restore recycled items.
   >
   > **Audio File 3:**
   > When creating folders keep in mind that you can create as many folders as you need.

2. Rehearse the audio script.

   ☐ using a measured (not too fast nor too slow) cadence, read the following out loud:

   Welcome to Super Simplistic Solutions learning series.

   This is lesson one: Creating New Folders.

   Next you'll record your voice in Camtasia. You can close the script now if you'd like.

3. Using Camtasia, open **NarrateMe** from the **Camtasia2023Data > Projects** folder.

4. Record voiceover audio.

   ☐ on the **Timeline**, position the Playhead on the **Lesson 1** group

   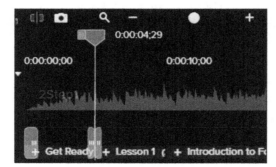

   ☐ from the tools at the left, click **Voice Narration**

On the **Voice Narration** panel, notice that I have already added the part of the voiceover script you'll be recording. Alternatively, you could print the script document and have it beside you during the recording phase.

☐ if necessary, select **your microphone** from the drop-down menu at the top of the Voice Narration panel

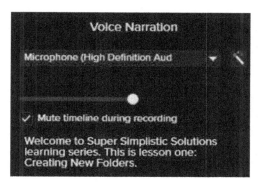

☐ ensure **Mute timeline during recording** is selected

Muting the Timeline is a good idea for this video because you have background audio on Track 2. If you don't mute the audio, the music could play through your computer speakers and ruin your voiceover audio.

And now, prepare yourself! Once you start the recording process, there isn't a count-down or any kind of warning. Instead, Camtasia simply starts recording. While you are recording, the video will play on the Canvas so you can see what's happening in your project while you narrate.

☐ click the **Start Voice Recording** button

There's a difference between the Mac and PC when it comes to recording audio. In the image above at the left, the Start Voice Recording button for PC users does not have a microphone icon. When finished recording audio on the PC, you are prompted to give the audio file a name. On the Mac, recorded audio is automatically saved and the media added to the Timeline.

☐ using a slow, deliberate cadence, read the following out loud:

Welcome to Super Simplistic Solutions learning series.

This is lesson one: Creating New Folders.

5. When finished, click the **Stop** button.

   PC users, the Save Narration As dialog box opens.
   Mac users, the audio is automatically saved and added to the Timeline.

6. PC users only: Name the file **My_Lesson1_Voiceover** and save it to the **Audio_Files** folder within the **Camtasia2023Data** folder.

NOTES

All users, your voiceover narration appears on a new track on the Timeline. In addition, the new audio has been added to the Media Bin.

7. Preview the project.

   You should be able to hear your new voiceover audio. However, notice that the audio is hard to hear because the background music is playing at the same time. You'll fix that shortly.

8. Save your work. (Mac users: You can close the project.)

Splitting Media

You will find Camtasia's ability to split media segments on the Timeline to be a valuable feature. Have you imported an audio clip that's too long and difficult to manage? Click at the top of Timeline where you want to split the audio clip and quickly split the clip into as many segments as you need. Want to add a transition in the middle of a video clip? Because transitions cannot be inserted in the middle of a clip, click where you need a transition and insert a split.

Guided Activity 33: Split Audio Media

1. Using Camtasia, open **SplitMe** from the **Camtasia2023Data > Projects** folder.

    This is basically the same project you were just working on except the voiceover audio that you recorded and inserted during the last activity has been replaced by a file named **audio_file01**.

2. Preview the project and notice, as mentioned at the end of the last activity, the background music and voiceover audio are playing at the same time, making it difficult to understand what the narrator is saying.

3. Lock Tracks.

    ☐ at the far left of the Timeline, click the padlock icon to the left of **Track 1** and **Track 3** to **lock** those tracks (only **Track 2** should remain unlocked)

    You are about to split the background music into two parts and then manipulate the two audio pieces on the Timeline so that they don't fight with the voiceover audio. During the splitting process, it's possible not only to split the background music but also to inadvertently split media in other tracks. Now that you have locked two of the three tracks, only the media in Track 2 (which is unlocked) will be affected.

4. Split the background music in Track 2 into two segments.

    ☐ on the **Timeline**, position the Playhead at the **4;29** mark

    ☐ on the **Timeline**, select the media in **Track 2**

    ☐ right-click the **Playhead** and choose **Split Selected**

    The music track is split into two parts (as shown in the second image above).

Audio Timing Confidence Check

1. Select the second (larger) segment of the background music.

2. Drag the **left edge** of the segment to the **right** until it lines up with the end of the **audio_file01** media in **Track 3**.

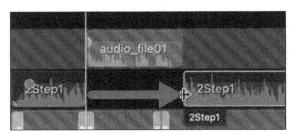

3. On Track 2, select the **first segment of the background music** and, using the **Audio Effects** panel, **Fade Out** the media.

4. On Track 2, select the **second segment of the background music** and **Fade In** the media.

5. Preview the project.

   The background music stops pretty much when the narrator begins to speak. Nice. The music does not start again until *after* the narrator is finished speaking.

   There's a problem now with the timing for Lesson 1 group. The group isn't on the Canvas quite long enough to match the voiceover audio. To fix that, you'll need to change the timing of a few Timeline objects.

6. Save your work. (Mac users: You can close the project.)

Audio Editing

Earlier in this module, you learned how to edit an audio clip by fading the volume in and out. Camtasia offers you other editing options, such as the ability to cut segments of a waveform and even to replace unwanted audio with silence.

Guided Activity 34: Rename Tracks

1. Open **EditMyAudio** from the **Camtasia2023Data > Projects** folder.

   This project is similar to the project you were just working on with a few notable exceptions. First, all of the tracks are unlocked. Second, two of the tracks, Voiceover and Background Audio, have names that are more descriptive than the default names Track 1, Track 2, etc. There's also additional voiceover audio in the Voiceover track.

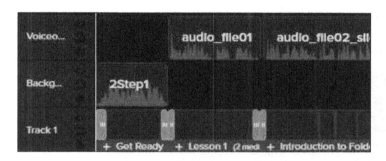

2. Rename a track.

   ☐ on the far left of the Timeline, double-click the name **Track 1**

   ☐ replace the text with the word **Main** and press [**enter**]

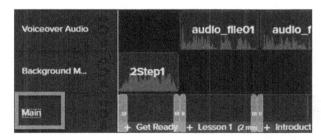

   While naming Timeline tracks is optional, I find it's a helpful step especially when dealing with larger projects that contain more than a few tracks.

NOTES

Guided Activity 35: Silence Audio, Delete, and Ripple Delete

1. Ensure that the **EditMyAudio** project is open.

2. Preview an audio clip.

   ☐ on the **Media Bin**, double-click **audio_file02_silence** to preview the media

   There are two strange sounds in the clip, and there's a bit of dead air at the end of the audio file. You have two choices for removing unwanted audio segments: delete the content or replace the content with **Silence**. When you delete the content, the media's duration is reduced by the amount of audio that is deleted. However, if your goal is to simply remove a problem in the audio clip (such as click sounds) without altering the duration of the media, using Silence is an ideal solution.

3. Close the media's **Preview** window.

4. Lock both the **Background** and **Main** tracks.

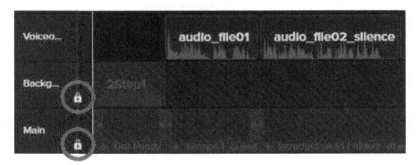

   As you learned earlier, locking a track ensures changes made to other unlocked tracks will not affect locked tracks.

5. Replace a selection of audio with silence.

   ☐ on the **Voiceover Audio** track, double-click **audio_file02_silence** to position the Playhead at the beginning of the audio file

   ☐ at the top of the **Timeline**, drag the **Zoom** slider right to zoom much closer to the Timeline

   At this enhanced view, you can get a better look at the waveform that makes up the audio file. You can see that the narrator's audio levels are consistent across the wave.

Take a look at about the **15 second** mark on the Timeline. There's a spike in the wave that isn't consistent with the rest of the wave. This part of the wave is an erroneous sound that you need to remove.

❑ position the **Playhead** to the beginning of the errant sound

❑ on the **Playhead**, drag the red box **right** to highlight the sound

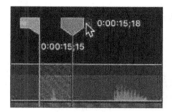

❑ on the **Timeline**, right-click the selection and choose **Silence Audio**

The errant sound is removed without altering the playtime of the media.

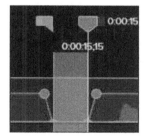

6. On the Timeline, double-click the Playhead.

   The green and red selection boxes on the Playhead snap back to the Playhead.

NOTES

NOTES

7. Delete selected media.

❑ on the **Timeline**, scroll **right** to the end of the **audio_file02_silence** media

There is **dead air** in the audio_file02_silence media that you can delete.

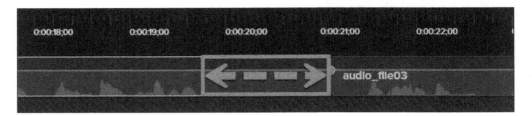

❑ on the **Timeline**, position the Playhead at **19;21** (this is the point in the media where the narrator is finished speaking and then there's dead air)

❑ drag the Playhead's red box to the **right** to highlight through the end of the **audio_file02_silence** media

❑ right-click the selection and choose **Delete** (PC) or **Delete Range** (Mac)

The selected portion of the audio clip is removed but you've now got **a sizable gap** on the Timeline. Instead of simply deleting a selection, you can delete both the content and the gap by using **Ripple Delete** instead of Delete.

8. Undo the last step.

❑ choose **Edit > Undo**

9. Ripple Delete selected media.

❑ ensure that the dead air is still selected in the **Voiceover** track

❑ PC users, right-click the selection and choose **Ripple Delete**
Mac users, right-click the selection and choose **Ripple Delete Range**

On the Timeline, the gap to the right of the deleted content is filled automatically by track content to the right of the selection.

Audio Editing Confidence Check

1. There's another errant sound at about the 16-second mark on the **Timeline**.

2. Select and then replace the sound with Silence.

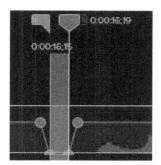

> **Note:** Remember to double-click the Playhead to return it to its default setting (the green and red boxes will snap back to the Playhead).

3. Save your work. (Mac users: You can close the project.)

Notes

iCONLOGiC

"Skills and Drills" Learning

Module 6: Exporting

In This Module You Will Learn About:

- Video and Web Output, page 104

And You Will Learn To:

- Export a Video on the Mac, page 104
- Export a Mac Project as a Website, page 107
- Export a Video on Windows, page 109
- Export a Windows Project as a Website, page 111
- Add a Watermark to Windows Projects, page 114
- Export to YouTube, page 118

Video and Web Output

As you have worked through the first several modules in this book, you learned how to record a video using the Recorder (page 22). Then, beginning on page 38, you learned how to add videos to the Editor. You added images (page 43), annotations/captions (page 64), behaviors/animations (page 74), and audio (page 85).

To create or edit eLearning with Camtasia, you need a licensed copy of Camtasia. When your project is finished, you export it as either a video, a website, audio, or an animated GIF. There are even options allowing you to export directly to media servers like Screencast, YouTube, Vimeo, and Google Drive. To be clear, your users do not need to have a copy of the Camtasia software to use your exported projects. Learners can use your content on devices such as desktop computers, laptops, and mobile devices (smart-phones, tablets, etc.).

You can export a standalone video that you can email to a learner or upload to a corporate server. The video can be opened by users via free utilities such as Media Player on the PC or QuickTime on the Mac. You can also export a project as a website that can be opened with any modern web browser. You can also export the project as a zipped content package for use within a Learning Management System (LMS).

During the next few activities, you will learn how to export your project as a standalone video and as a website. The process of exporting is very different for Mac and PC users. First up, Mac users. PC users can skip ahead to page 109.

Guided Activity 36: Export a Video on the Mac

1. Using Camtasia, open **ExportMe** from the **Camtasia2023Data > Projects** folder.

2. Produce the video for the web.

   ☐ choose **Export > Local File**

   The Export As dialog box opens.

   ☐ change the **Export As** name to **Create_Folders_MP4_Only**

   ☐ navigate to the **Camtasia2023Data > Produced_Videos** folder

   ☐ from the **File format** drop-down menu at the bottom of the dialog box, choose **Export to MP4 (.mp4)**

   ☐ click the **Export** button

The project exports. You can track the export progress via the dialog box shown below. While your project is exporting, you won't be able to work within Camtasia without first canceling the export process.

Once the export process is complete, you'll see the **Export finished** dialog box.

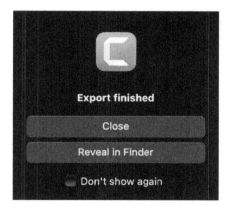

☐ click the **Reveal in Finder** button

The Produced Videos folder opens. The only file in the folder at this point is the single video that you just exported.

3. Open the video file in a media player.

☐ right-click (or [**control**] click) the video and choose **Always Open With > QuickTime Player.app**

The published video opens in your computer's media player.

☐ click the **Play** button on the playbar to start the video

I don't know about you, but I think this whole export process went just a bit too smoothly. I bet you're thinking that I set this project up in advance so that when you exported this particular project, things would go perfectly. And I'm betting that you're betting that once you try to do this on your own, the wheels are going to come off of your cart and nothing is going to work as smoothly as it just did.

Let me assure you that the export process you just worked through was based on default settings you'll find in Camtasia "out of the box." There was nothing in the ExportMe video set up in advance to ensure success in the export process. In fact, you can run through the same export process using any Camtasia project, and the result should be the same as those shown in this activity.

You will get a chance to play with some of the other Export options in a bit. For now, enjoy your progress. Believe it or not, you are now a published eLearning author. Congratulations!

4. Close the media player and return to the Camtasia project.

Guided Activity 37: Export a Mac Project as a Website

1. Ensure that the **ExportMe** project is open.

2. Export the project as a Web Page.

   ☐ choose **Export > Local File**

   ☐ change the **Export as** name to **ExportMe_Web_Version**

   ☐ if necessary, navigate to the **Camtasia2023Data > Produced_Videos** folder

   ☐ from the **File format** drop-down menu at the bottom of the dialog box, choose **Export to MP4 (.mp4)**

   ☐ from beneath the **Caption Style** area, select **Export as Web Page**

   ☐ click the **Export** button

3. Once the Export process is complete, click the **Reveal in Finder** button.

   The last time you exported the project, you exported the project as a video. And once the video was exported, the process yielded a single file. This time, you've created a website with assets that rely on each other to correctly work in a browser. When you upload these assets to a web server, the assets must be kept together.

4. Open the **ExportMe_Web_Version** folder.

   There's a single html file in the folder: **index.html**. This is the start page for the lesson. There is also a media folder containing several required assets.

5. View the exported project in a web browser.

    ❐ from within the **ExportMe_Web_Version** folder, double-click **index.html**

    The rendered project opens in your default web browser.

    ❐ click the **Play** button in the middle of the screen to play the lesson

6. When finished, close the browser window.

7. Return to the Camtasia project.

    The next few activities are for PC users only. Mac users, skip ahead to the "Export to YouTube" activity on page 118.

Guided Activity 38: Export a Video on Windows

1. Using Camtasia, open **ExportMe** from the **Camtasia2023Data > Projects** folder.

2. Export the project as a video.

   ☐ choose **Export > Local File**

   The Export Local File dialog box opens.

   ☐ change the **File name** to **ExportMe_MP4_Only**
   ☐ from the **File Type** menu, ensure that **MP4** is selected
   ☐ from the **Save location** area, click the **Browse** icon
   ☐ from the **Camtasia2023Data** folder, open the **Produced_Videos** folder
   ☐ click the **Select Folder** button

   ☐ click the **Export** button

   The Exporting Project screen opens allowing you to track the export process. Generally speaking, the longer the playtime of your video and the more video and audio media added to the Timeline, the longer the exporting process will take to complete.

   Once the export process is complete, the Exporter screen opens. You can close the Exporter, view the output, or locate the exported video file.

NOTES

☐ click the **Open File Location** button

The **Produced_Videos** folder contains a single video file.

☐ ExportMe_MP4_Only.mp4

☐ double-click the video file

The video opens in your default video player and begins to play.

I don't know about you, but I think this whole export process went just a bit too smoothly. I bet you're thinking that I set this project up in advance so that when you exported this particular project, things would go perfectly. And I'm betting that you're betting that once you try to do this on your own, the wheels are going to come off of your cart and nothing is going to work as smoothly as it just did.

Let me assure you that the export process you just worked through was based on default settings you'll find in Camtasia "out of the box." There was nothing in the ExportMe video set up in advance to ensure success in the export process. In fact, you can run through the same export process using any Camtasia project, and the result should be the same as those shown in this activity.

You will get a chance to play with some of the other Export options in a bit. For now, enjoy your progress. Believe it or not, you are now a published eLearning author. Congratulations!

3. Close the media player.

Guided Activity 39: Export a Windows Project as a Website

1. Back in Camtasia, ensure that the **ExportMe** project is open.

2. Produce a video for the web that includes the Smart Player.

   ☐ choose **Export > Legacy Local File**

   The Production Wizard opens.

   ☐ from the drop-down menu, choose **MP4 with Smart Player (up to 720p)**

   ☐ click the **Next** button
   ☐ change the **Production Name** to ExportMe_HMTL5
   ☐ from the **Folder** area, click the **Browse** icon
   ☐ from the **Camtasia2023Data** folder, open the **Produced_Videos** folder
   ☐ click the **Save** button

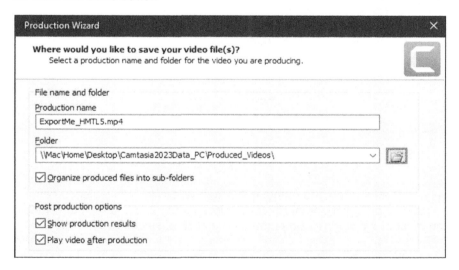

   ☐ click the **Finish** button

   The Rendering Project screen opens.

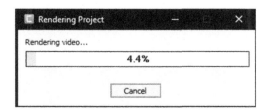

   Unlike the video output, the rendered output does not open in your Media Player like last time. This time, you have output a website and the start page automatically opens in your default Web browser.

☐ click the **Play** button in the middle of the screen to play the lesson

The Smart Player appears at the bottom of the window every time you move your mouse within the browser window. The player automatically disappears when you move your mouse away from the browser window.

3. Close the browser window and return to Camtasia.

4. On the Production Results screen, click the **Open production folder** button.

When you export as a video, the output is a single video file. While videos cannot be interactive beyond providing the ability for the learner to play, pause, and rewind, videos will play on most of the world's computers and mobile devices.

When you export as MP4 with Smart Player, you end up with several co-dependent files. This kind of output includes HTML files, videos, and support files that will play in any modern web browser and on most devices including desktop computers, laptops, tablets and smartphones.

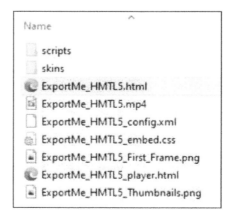

Be aware of a specific file in the output folder: *the start page*. The start page is always given the name you used when you exported. The start page in your output folder is called **ExportMe_HTML5.html**.

Although all of the files in this folder are co-dependent and must be uploaded to the server, the start page is the page your learners need to start the exported lesson. If you are working with a webmaster or IT support, they need to understand the importance of keeping these files together *and* making the start page the target of any links to the course content within the folder you rendered.

5. Close the window and return to Camtasia.

6. Back in Camtasia, click the **Finish** button to close the **Production Results** screen.

Guided Activity 40: Add a Watermark to Windows Projects

1. Ensure that the **ExportMe** project is open.

2. Export using Custom production settings.

   ☐ choose **Export > Legacy Local File**

   The Production Wizard opens.

   ☐ select **Custom production settings** from the drop-down menu

   ☐ click the **Next** button
   ☐ if necessary, select **MP4 - Smart Player (HTML5)**

   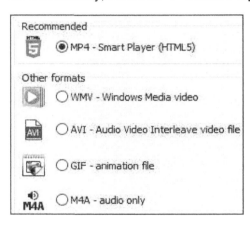

   ☐ click the **Next** button

   The Smart Player Options appear.

3. Edit the HTML Title.

   ☐ click the **Options** tab
   ☐ in the HTML title area, change the title to **Working with Folders**

   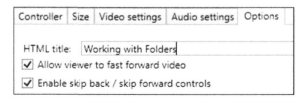

   The HTML title appears in the web browser tab when the lesson is opened by a learner.

   ☐ click the **Next** button

   The Video Options open.

4. Add a watermark.

   ☐ from the **Watermark** area, select **Include watermark**

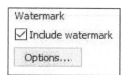

   ☐ click the **Options** button just below **Include watermark**

The Watermark options appear along with a Watermark Preview window.

   ☐ click the **Browse** button at the right (the yellow folder)
   ☐ from the **Camtasia2023Data > Image_Files** folder, open **ForReviewOnly**

The image appears, by default, in the lower right of the Watermark Preview.

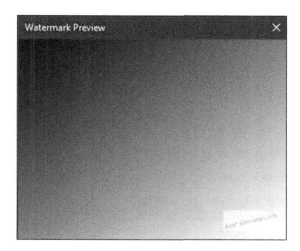

5. Change the position of the watermark.

   ☐ from the **Position** area, click the **top right** square (you may need to move the **Watermark Preview** window out of the way to see the Position area)

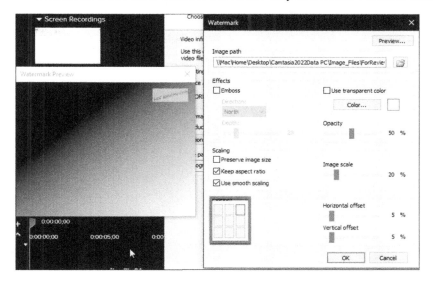

6. Remove the watermark's background color.

   ❏ from the **Effects** area, select **Use transparent color**

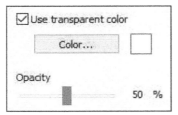

   The background color behind the logo watermark has been removed.

7. Change the Image scale.

   ❏ from the **Image scale** area, drag the slider until the scale changes to **30%**

   ❏ click the **OK** button to return to the Production Wizard
   ❏ click the **Next** button to move to the final screen

8. Give the rendered video a new production name.

   ❏ change the **Production name** to **ExportMe_watermark**
   ❏ ensure the output folder is **Produced_Videos**

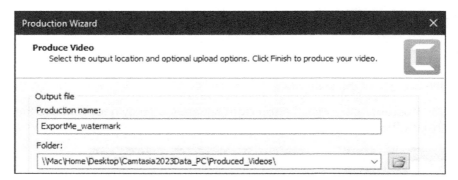

   ❏ click the **Finish** button

The exported project opens in your default web browser, including the watermark.

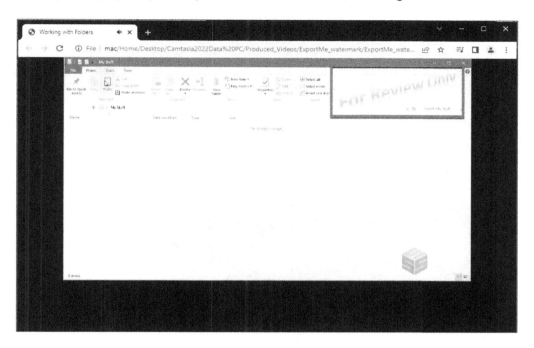

Notice that the HTML title you added appears in the browser's title area. (You added the HTML Title on page 114.)

9. Close the browser.

10. Back in Camtasia, close the Production Results dialog box (click the **Finish** button).

11. Save your work.

Guided Activity 41: Export to YouTube

1. Ensure that the **ExportMe** project is open.

   Before you can export a video to YouTube, you need a YouTube account. If you do not already have a YouTube or Gmail account, go to **www.youtube.com** or **gmail.com** now and set one up. Creating an account takes only a few moments and is free.

2. Export a video directly to YouTube.

   ☐ choose **Export > YouTube**

   You'll be prompted to Sign in to your YouTube account.

   ☐ click the **Sign In** button and then follow the onscreen prompts to access your YouTube account

3. Give the video a Title, Description, and Tags (keywords).

   ☐ in the **Title** field, type **Creating New Folders**

   ☐ in the **Description** field, type **This demonstration will teach you how to create a folder using Windows.**

   ☐ in the **Tags** field, type **training, windows, file management**

   The tags make it easier for YouTube users to search YouTube and find your video.

   ☐ leave the **Privacy** option set to **Public (anyone can search and view)**

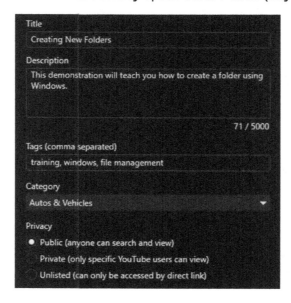

4. Export the video.

   ☐ click the **Finish** button

   The video is rendered and automatically posted to your YouTube account.

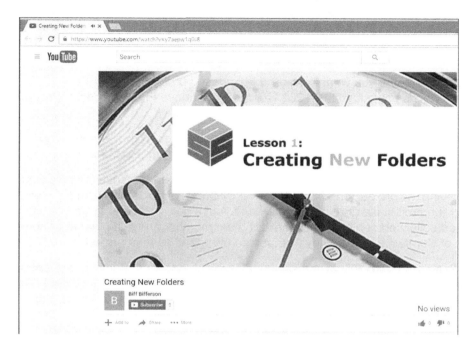

5. Close the web browser and return to Camtasia.

Sharing Projects Confidence Check

If you work with other Camtasia developers, it's likely that you will be asked to share your project with team members so they can edit the project. Sharing projects among Camtasia developers is not the same as using the Export menu to create output for a learner as you've learned to do during this module.

To share Camtasia production files with other Camtasia developers, follow these steps:

Mac to Windows: If you want to share a Mac-based project with someone who is using Camtasia 2023 for the PC, choose **File > Export > Project for Windows**.

Windows to Mac: If you want to share a PC-based project with someone who is using Camtasia 2023 for the Mac, choose **File > Export > Project for Mac**.

Share Projects Mac to Mac: Sharing a project with other Mac developers is simple. When saving the project, ensure that you select **Create standalone project**. Send a team member the project file (the **cmproj** file), and you're set. The **cmproj** file is a self-contained collection of all project assets. If team members have the same or newer version of Camtasia as you, they'll be able to open and edit the project.

Share Projects PC to PC: When saving the project, ensure that you select **Create standalone project**.Send the resulting folder to the other Camtasia developer. The folder will likely contain several assets so zipping the project is suggested. Those steps follow.

Note: The steps below are for PC users only. Mac users can save and close the project and then skip ahead to the next module which begins on page 121.

1. Choose **File > Export > Zipped Project**.

2. Browse to a save destination of your choice.

3. Click the **Save** button.

   The resulting zip file contains the Camtasia project and all of the project's assets. Assuming the recipient of the zip file has the same version of Camtasia as you, developers can extract the contents, open, edit, and export the project.

4. Save the project.

iCONLOGiC
"Skills and Drills" Learning

Module 7: Extending, Zooming, and Hotspots

In This Module You Will Learn About:

- Extending, page 122
- Zoom Animations, page 124
- Markers, page 128
- Hotspots, page 131

And You Will Learn To:

- Extend a Video Frame, page 122
- Add a Zoom-n-Pan Animation on the PC, page 124
- Add a Zoom Animation on the Mac, page 126
- Add a Timeline Marker, page 128
- Add an Interactive Hotspot, page 131

Extending

If you record a software demonstration and then audio, as you've done several times during the previous activities, synchronizing the video with the audio can be challenging. During the following activity, you'll learn how to freeze a video on a single frame, making synchronization easier.

Guided Activity 42: Extend a Video Frame

1. Open the **ExtendZoomMe** project.

2. On the **Timeline**, notice that **audio_file07** has been added to the Timeline at the **2:26;00 second mark**, above the **RestoreFolder** media.

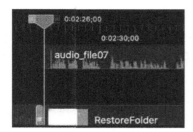

3. Beginning at **2:26;00** on the **Timeline**, preview the project.

   In the video, the narrator is talking about the Recycle Bin and how its appearance has changed to indicate there's trash to be emptied. The video is just a bit ahead of the voiceover audio. Rather than re-record the video, you're going to freeze the video just long enough to synchronize the voiceover audio with the video.

4. Lock the **Voiceover** and **Background** tracks.

   As you first learned on page 95, locking tracks prevents accidental changes. The media you are about to modify is on the Main track and you do not want to alter the other tracks.

5. Split a video into two segments.

   ☐ on the **Timeline**, zoom closer

   ☐ on the **Timeline**, drag the **Playhead** a bit right to **2:26;16**

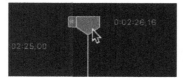

   This is the point in the video just before the cursor moves toward the Recycle Bin.

❑ on the **Timeline**, **Main** track, select the **RestoreFolder** media

❑ right-click the **Playhead** and choose **Split Selected**

The video has been split into two segments. One of the segments is significantly larger than the other.

6. Reposition a video segment.

❑ on the **Timeline**, position the **Playhead** at **2:29;05**

❑ on the **Timeline**, drag the **larger** of the two video segments **right** until it snaps to the Playhead's position at **2:29;05**

The gap between the two video segments is going to be filled by extending the last frame in the smaller segment.

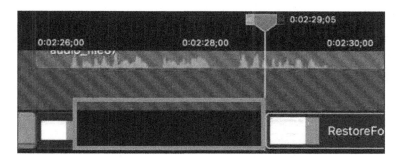

❑ double-click the **smaller video segment** to both select the media and move the Playhead in front of the media segment

❑ on your keyboard, press [**alt**] (PC) or [**option**] (Mac) and **drag** the **right edge** of the smaller video media right until it snaps to the larger segment

7. Preview from the beginning of the first RestoreFolder media.

Extending the frame has made the video freeze just long enough to allow the screen actions and voiceover audio to synchronize.

NOTES

Zoom Animations

The Zoom-n-Pan feature is useful if the width and height of your project are large and you want to focus the learner's attention on a specific area of the screen. Zooming moves the learner closer to the screen; Panning automatically moves the screen for the learner. Adding Zooms and Pans is as simple as positioning the Playhead where you want to add the effect, accessing the Zoom-n-Pan panel (via Animations) and stretching and/or moving the Zoom-n-Pan window.

> **Note:** The next activity is for PC users only. Mac users, your steps can be found on page 126.

Guided Activity 43: Add a Zoom-n-Pan Animation on the PC

1. Ensure that the **ExtendZoomMe** project is open.

2. Add a Zoom-n-Pan mark.

   ☐ on the **Timeline**, unlock the locked tracks (you locked the Background Music and Voiceover Audio tracks earlier)

   ☐ on the **Timeline**, position the Playhead at **0:47;27**

   On the Canvas, this is when the cursor has arrived at the Home tab and is about to click.

   ☐ from the list of tools at the left, click **Animations**

   There are two tabs: **Zoom-n-Pan** and **Animations**.

   ☐ select the **Zoom-n-Pan** tab

   ☐ on the **Zoom-n-Pan** panel, drag the lower right resizing handle **up** and to the **left** similar to the picture below

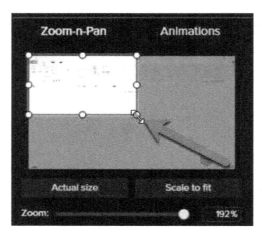

When you drag the resizing handle on the Zoom-n-Pan panel, the Canvas displays how close you've actually gotten to the screen.

On the Timeline, notice that the effect is represented by an arrow with two circles. You can change the zoom percentage by selecting the larger circle and changing the Scale on the Properties panel.

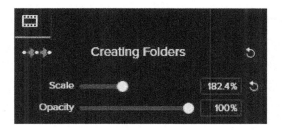

3. On the **Timeline**, position the **Playhead** a few seconds to the left of the zoom effect you just added.

4. Preview the project.

   Thanks to the Zoom-n-Pan, you are automatically zoomed closer to the action in the video.

5. Save your work.

   The next activity is for Mac users only. PC users, skip ahead to the "Add a Timeline Marker" activity that begins on page 128.

Guided Activity 44: Add a Zoom Animation on the Mac

1. Ensure that the **ExtendZoomMe** project is open.

2. Add a Zoom-n-Pan mark.

   ☐ on the **Timeline**, unlock the locked tracks

   ☐ position the Playhead at **47;27**

   This is the area of the video where the mouse pointer has arrived at the Home tab and is about to click.

   ☐ from the list of tools at the left, click **Animations**

   ☐ from the list of Animations, drag the **Custom** animation to the **Creating Folders** group on the **Timeline**

   ☐ position the animation on the **Creating Folders** group at **47;27**

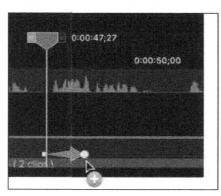

   On the Timeline, notice that the animation is represented by an arrow with two circles (one circle is at the head, one is positioned at the tail). The circle on the tail represents the beginning of the animation. The circle at the head represents the end of the animation. You can change the zoom percentage by selecting the tail or the head and changing the Scale on the Properties panel.

   ☐ on the **Timeline**, select the animation's head at **48;27** (the larger circle)

☐ on the **Properties** panel, change the **Scale** to **200**

☐ on the **Canvas**, drag the video down and to the right so you can see the top left of the video

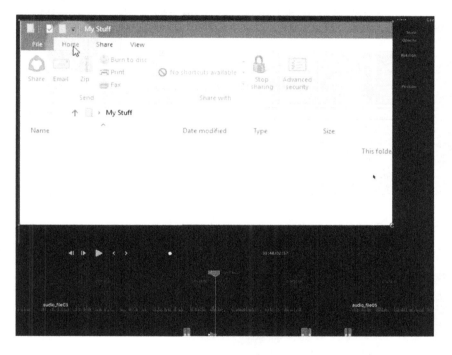

3. On the **Timeline**, position the **Playhead** a few seconds to the left of the zoom Animation you just edited.

4. Preview the project.

   Thanks to the animation, you are automatically taken closer to the action in the video.

5. Save your work and close the project.

Markers

Markers are project-wide breadcrumbs that can be added to the Timeline or Timeline objects. Markers are the key to Camtasia's interactive features, such as a table of contents, closed captions, hotspot functionality, and quizzing.

Guided Activity 45: Add a Timeline Marker

1. Open the **MarkMe** project.

    On the Timeline, notice that there are some additional tracks: **Nav1**, **Nav2**, and **Nav3**. The tracks contain shapes at Timeline position **03;24**.

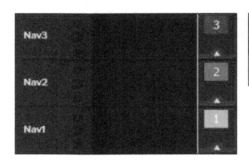

2. Add and rename a Timeline Marker.

    ☐ on the **Timeline**, position the **Playhead** at **00;23**

    ☐ choose **Modify > Markers > Add Timeline Marker**

    On the Timeline, a marker is added just below the Playhead. On the Properties panel, the new marker is named **Marker**.

    ☐ on the **Properties** panel, change the **Marker name** to **Home** and press [**enter**]

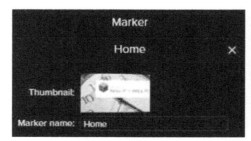
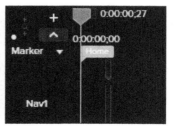

Markers and TOC Confidence Check

1. Still working in the **MarkMe** project, position the **Playhead** just after the transition for the **Lesson 1** group (05;15).

2. Add a new Timeline marker (**Modify > Markers > Add Timeline Marker**) named **Lesson 1: Creating New Folders**.

3. Position the Playhead just after the transition for the **Lesson 2** group. (01:03;28)

4. Add a new Timeline marker named **Lesson 2: Renaming Folders**.

5. Position the Playhead just after the transition for the **Lesson 3** group.

6. Add a new Timeline marker named **Lesson 3: Recycling and Restoring**. (01:45;23)

   The Timeline should now have four markers.

TechSmith provides a free hosting service called Screencast where you can upload your Camtasia and Snagit output. Screencast is especially useful if you do not have a LMS or web server where you can host your output. You will need to create an account on Screencast prior to finishing this Confidence Check. If you do not have an account, go to **https://app.screencast.com/** and set one up prior to moving to the next step.

7. Export the project to **Screencast** by choosing **Export > Screencast**.

8. Title the course **Working_with_Folders**.

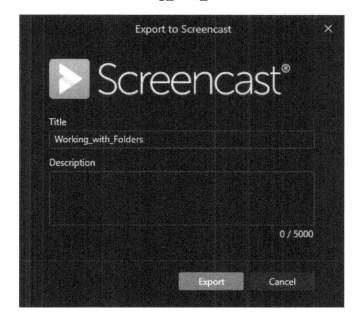

9. Click **Export** (PC) or **Share** (Mac).

   PC users, the output should open in Screencast automatically. Mac users: Click the **Visit** button to see the output on Screencast.

On Screencast, the Table of Contents can be viewed by clicking the icon on the playbar at the bottom of the lesson. On the TOC, you can click any of the thumbnails to jump to the Timeline markers.

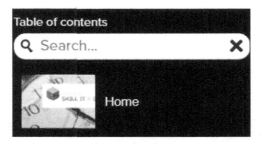

Note: If the TOC does not work for you, try copying the web address in the browser's address bar and pasting it into the address bar within a different browser. On my Mac, Chrome tends to work better than Safari.

10. Close the browser and return to Camtasia.

11. Close all open windows and save your work. (Mac users, you can save and close any open projects.)

Hotspots

To maximize the effectiveness of your eLearning videos, you can use hotspots to add interactivity. The hotspots can pause the video and wait for a click from your learner. Once clicked, a hotspot can be set up to take the learner to a marker, a website, or a specific time on the Timeline.

Guided Activity 46: Add an Interactive Hotspot

1. Open the **HotSpotMe** project.

    There are three shapes on the Canvas and at the beginning of the Timeline in the **Nav1**, **Nav2**, and **Nav3** tracks. You're going to use a hotspot to make each shape interactive.

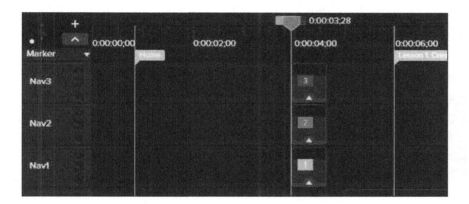

2. Add an Interactive Hotspot to an object on the Canvas.

    ☐ zoom a bit closer to the **Timeline**

    ☐ on the **Timeline**, **Nav1** track, double-click the **green shape** at **03;28**

    The green annotation containing the number **1** is displayed on the Canvas and selected.

    ☐ from the tools at the left, click **Visual Effects**

    ☐ right-click **Interactive Hotspot** and choose **Add to Selected Media**

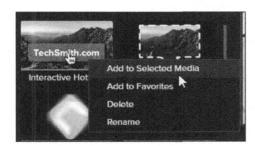

NOTES

If alerted that "Hotspots work best with a duration of at least 1 second," click the **OK** button. While it's generally a good idea to ensure a duration of 1 second or more, in this instance the effect will work just fine.

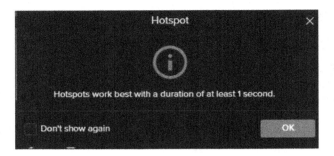

3. Add an Action to a Hotspot.

   ☐ on the **Properties** panel, **Interactive Hotspot** section, ensure **Pause at end** is selected

   This option ensures that the video doesn't move forward without giving the learner a chance to interact with the shape.

   ☐ on the **Properties** panel, **Interactive Hotspot** section, select **Marker**

   ☐ from the **Marker** drop-down menu, choose the **Lesson 1: Creating New Folders** marker (you learned how to create this particular marker on page 128)

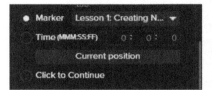

Interactive Hotspot Confidence Check

1. Add an Interactive Hotspot to the red annotation in the Nav2 track.

2. Make the target of the hotspot the **Lesson 2** marker.

3. Add an Interactive Hotspot to the annotation in the Nav3 track.

4. Make the target of the hotspot the **Lesson 3** marker.

5. Export the project to **Screencast** with the Title **Working_with_Folders_Hotspots**.

6. Visit the lesson on Screencast and test the hotspots.

7. When finished, close the browser and then return to Camtasia.

8. Save your work. (Mac users, you can close the project.)

iCONLOGiC

"Skills and Drills" Learning

Module 8: Quizzes and Reporting Results

In This Module You Will Learn About:

- Quizzes, page 134
- Reporting Quiz Results, page 141

And You Will Learn To:

- Add a Quiz to a Project, page 134
- Add a Multiple Choice Question, page 136
- Add a Fill In the Blank Question, page 138
- Create a Content Package on the PC, page 141
- Create a Content Package on the Mac, page 144

Quizzes

Many people compare the potential effectiveness of eLearning to live training. But it's not a fair comparison because eLearning lacks live, human interaction. In an instructor-led class, be it virtual or onsite, an experienced trainer can gauge the effectiveness of a lesson by asking the learner a question about something taught in the class. When a trainer asks questions, the learner has an opportunity to share what was learned and to demonstrate comprehension.

Although an eLearning lesson cannot provide live trainer-to-learner interaction, you can still engage the learner by adding quizzes to a Camtasia project. A quiz can contain any or all of the following question types: Multiple choice, True/False, Fill in the blank, and Short answer.

Guided Activity 47: Add a Quiz to a Project

1. Open the **QuizMe** project.

2. Add a quiz to the Timeline.

   ☐ on the **Timeline**, position the **Playhead** just after the last group (at **2:57;17**)

   ☐ choose **View > Show Quiz Track**

   A Quiz Track is added along the top of the Timeline.

   ☐ position your cursor on the Quiz Track just beneath the Playhead (which you positioned at **2:57;17**

   A green plus sign appears above the cursor. The icon indicates the location of a quiz.

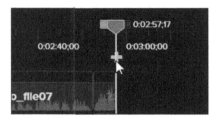

   ☐ click one time in the **Quiz Track** to add the quiz

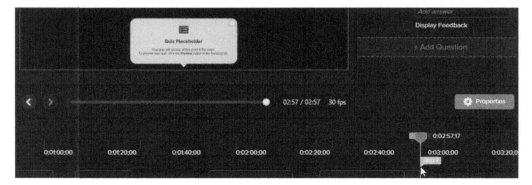

3. Rename the quiz.

☐ on the **Properties** panel, click **Quiz Options** (it's called **Quiz Option Properties** on the Mac, as shown in the second image below)

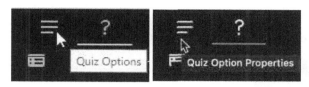

☐ change the Quiz Name to **Folders Quiz**

4. Ensure that the quiz will score the quiz questions.

☐ from just above the **Preview** button, ensure that **Viewers can see their results** is selected

☐ from just above the **Preview** button, ensure that **Score Quiz** is selected

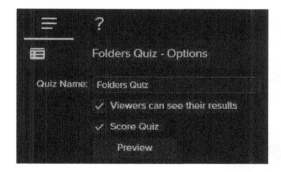

Guided Activity 48: Add a Multiple Choice Question

1. Ensure that the **QuizMe** project is open.

2. Add a Multiple Choice question to the quiz.

   ☐ on the **Properties** panel, click **Quiz Question Properties**

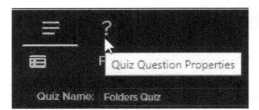

   ☐ from the **Type** drop-down menu, choose **Multiple Choice**

3. Type the question text.

   ☐ in the Question area, replace the placeholder text with **When giving a folder a name, how many characters can you use?**

4. Add four answers to the question.

   ☐ in the first **Answer** area, type **9**

   ☐ in the next **Answer** area, type **255**

   ☐ in the next **Answer** area, type **11**

   ☐ in the next **Answer** area, type **218**

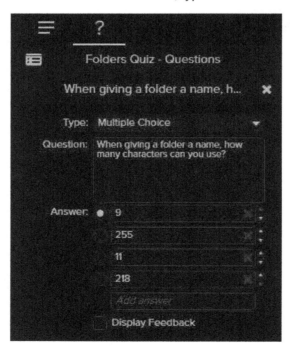

Note: There is an extra "*Add answer*" placeholder. Unless you type something into the placeholder, the answer will not appear in the quiz.

5. Specify a correct answer.

☐ click the circle to the left of the second answer, **255**

6. Save your work.

Guided Activity 49: Add a Fill In the Blank Question

1. Ensure that the **QuizMe** project is open.

2. Add a question.

   ☐ on the **Properties** panel, click **Add Question**

   Note: You may need to scroll down a bit to see the Add Question area.

   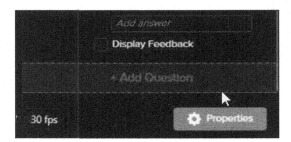

   The new question appears below the first.

3. Specify the question type.

   ☐ from the **Type** drop-down menu, choose **Fill in the Blank**

4. Edit the Question.

   ☐ replace the **Question Text** placeholder text with **The New Folder icon is found on the _____ tab of the Ribbon.**

5. Edit the Answer.

   ☐ in the **Answer** area, replace the placeholder text with **Home**

   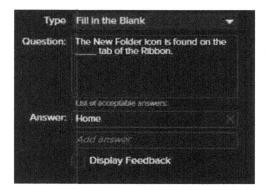

6. Save your work.

Quiz Confidence Check

1. Preview the quiz by clicking **See how Quiz looks in your viewer**. (On the Mac, the option is called **Preview quiz** as shown in the second image below.)

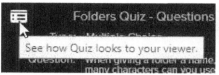  

A preview of the quiz appears on the Canvas.

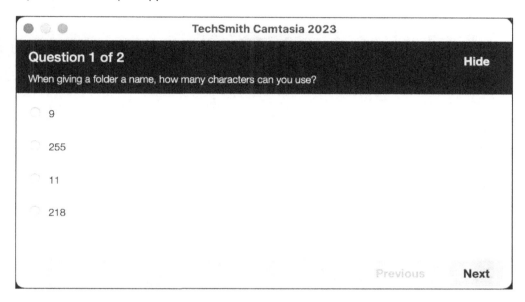

2. Select any of the answers in the first question and click the **Next** button (you'll likely need to scroll down to see the Next button).

3. Type anything you'd like into the text field within the **Fill in the Blank** question and then click the **Submit Answers** button.

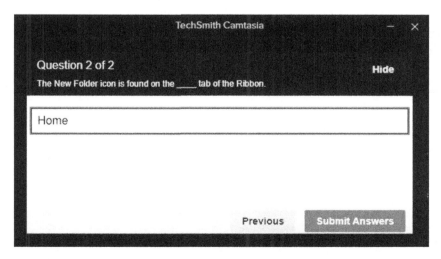

4. Click the **View Answers** button.

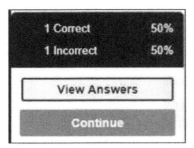

Correct answers are shown with a green check mark. Wrong answers are flagged with a red X.

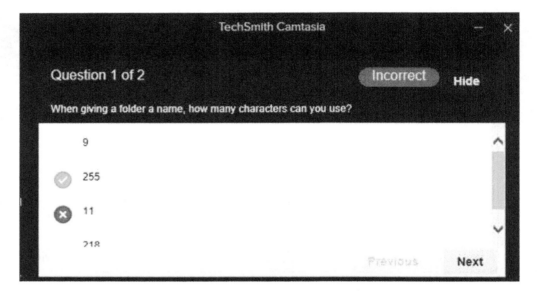

5. Close the Quiz preview.

6. Save the project. (Mac users, you can also close the project.)

Reporting Quiz Results

Earlier in this module, you uploaded content to Screencast and had the quiz results emailed to you. As an alternative to tracking quiz results through email, most eLearning developers upload their training courses into a Learning Management System (LMS). At a minimum, an LMS tracks learner access to the content, delivery of the content, and student performance tracking/reporting. Camtasia projects can be set up to report quiz scores to an LMS.

Before moving forward, I'd like to introduce you to two important terms: SCORM and Manifests.

SCORM

SCORM is an acronym for Sharable Content Object Reference Model. Developed by public- and private-sector organizations, SCORM is a series of standards that specify ways to catalog, launch, and track course objects.

Courses and management systems that follow the SCORM specifications allow for sharing of courses among federal agencies, colleges, and universities. Although SCORM is not the only sharing standard, it is one of the most common. There are two primary versions of SCORM, both available in Camtasia: version 1.2, released in 1999, and version 2004.

Manifests

A Manifest allows your exported output to be used and launched from a SCORM-compliant LMS. When you export a Camtasia project, you can have Camtasia create the Manifest file for you. The Manifest file that Camtasia creates contains XML tags that describe the organization and structure of the published project to the LMS.

During the activities that follow, you will create a content package, including a manifest file, suitable for upload into any SCORM-compliant LMS. The steps are different enough between the PC and Mac that I've split them up. PC users, you're up first below. Mac users, skip to page 144 for your steps to success.

Guided Activity 50: Create a Content Package on the PC

1. Open the **ReportMe** project.

   On the **Quiz Track** of the Timeline, notice that this project includes a quiz.

2. Enable SCORM reporting.

   ☐ choose **Export > Legacy Local File**

   ☐ choose **Custom Production Settings** from the drop-down menu

   ☐ click **Next** four times to advance to the **Quiz Reporting Options** screen

   ☐ select **Report quiz results using SCORM**

   > ☑ Report quiz results using SCORM
   >
   > Quiz appearance...

3. Set up the Manifest file.

   ☐ at the right of the dialog box, click the **SCORM Options** button

   The Manifest Options dialog box opens.

☐ leave the **Identifier** unchanged

You should only change the identifier if specifically instructed to do so by your LMS administrator.

☐ change the Course information **Title** to **Computer Basics**

☐ add the following **Description** text: **This course will teach you everything you ever wanted to know about computers but were afraid to ask.**

☐ change the **SCORM version** to **1.2**

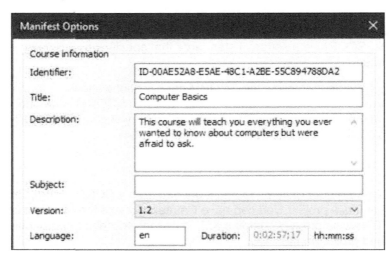

Some LMSs support SCORM version 1.2; some support only 2004, while others support both. Although it's typically a safe bet to go with SCORM 1.2, discuss the ideal version with your LMS vendor.

☐ change the Lesson information **Title** to **Creating, Renaming, and Recycling Folders**

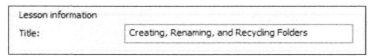

☐ from the **Quiz success** area, set the **Passing Score** to **50%**

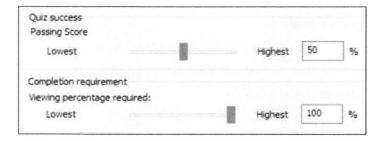

You have only two questions in your quiz, so a 50% pass setting seems about right.

☐ from the **SCORM Package options** area, select **Produce zip file**

SCORM Package options
⦿ Produce zip file
◯ Produce unzipped files
◯ Produce both zip file and unzipped files

☐ click the **OK** button

You should be back on the Production Wizard.

☐ click the **Next** button

☐ change the Output file name to **ReportMeSCORM**

☐ ensure that the output folder is the **Camtasia2023Data_PC > Produced_Videos**

Output file
Production name:

ReportMeSCORM

Folder:

\Camtasia2023Data_PC\Produced_Videos   ⌄   🗁

☑ Organize produced files into sub-folders

Post production options
☑ Show production results

☐ click the **Finish** button

4. Once the rendering process is complete, click the **Open production folder** button.

   The zipped content package has been created, ready for you to upload into any SCORM-compliant LMS.

   📦 ReportMeSCORM.zip

5. Close all windows.

6. Back in Camtasia, click the **Finish** button to close the Production results dialog box.

   The remaining steps in this module are for Mac users. You can move to the "PowerPoint, Captions, and Templates" module which begins on page 147.

Guided Activity 51: Create a Content Package on the Mac

1. Ensure that the **ReportMe** project is still open.

2. Enable SCORM reporting.

   ☐ choose **Export > Local File**

   ☐ change the **Export As** file name to **ReportMeSCORM**

   ☐ from beneath the **Caption Style** area, ensure **Include Quiz** is selected

   ☐ from beneath the **Caption Style** area, select **Include SCORM**

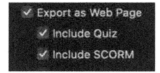

3. Set up the Manifest file.

   ☐ to the right of **Include SCORM**, click the **Options** button

   The Manifest Options dialog box opens.

   ☐ change the **Course Title** to **Computer Basics**

   ☐ add the following **Description** text: **This course will teach you everything you ever wanted to know about computers but were afraid to ask.**

   ☐ change the **SCORM version** to **1.2**

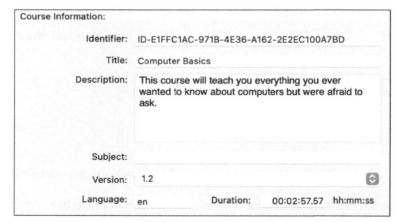

Some LMSs support SCORM version 1.2; some support only 2004, while others support both. Although it's typically a safe bet to go with SCORM 1.2, discuss the ideal version with your LMS vendor.

❑ change the **Lesson Title** to **Creating, Renaming, and Recycling Folders**

❑ from the **Quiz Success** area, set the Passing Score to **50%**

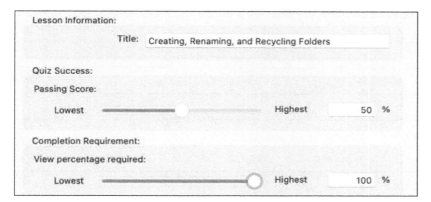

You have only two questions in your quiz, so a 50% pass setting seems about right.

❑ from the **SCORM Package options** area, select **Produce zip file**

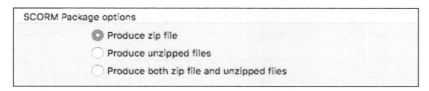

❑ click the **OK** button

❑ click the **Export** button

4. Once the Export process is complete, click the **Reveal in Finder** button.

The zipped content package has been created, ready for you to upload into an LMS.

5. Close all windows.

6. Back in Camtasia, save and close the project.

Notes

iCONLOGiC
"Skills and Drills" Learning

Module 9: PowerPoint, Captions, and Templates

In This Module You Will Learn About:

And You Will Learn To:

PowerPoint to Camtasia

I frequently meet eLearning developers who have created perfectly good Microsoft PowerPoint presentations, and they'd like to use those presentations as eLearning. Unfortunately, PowerPoint does not have the ability to add quizzes, create SCORM packages, or automatically upload content to YouTube or Screencast. Rather than try to recreate the PowerPoint presentation from scratch in Camtasia, you have two ways to re-purpose existing PowerPoint content in Camtasia. PC users can record a PowerPoint presentation from within PowerPoint using a Camtasia Add-in. The finished recording will end up in a Camtasia project as a video on the Timeline. From there, you can add all of the awesome Camtasia-specific features to the project that you've learned about in this book. Mac users cannot record a PowerPoint presentation from within PowerPoint because there isn't a Camtasia Recorder Add-in for the Mac version of PowerPoint. You can get around this limitation by recording your presentation using Camtasia's screen recorder (you learned how to use the Recorder on page 22).

Another option is to bring some or all the PowerPoint slides into Camtasia as images. Those images, which will be imported into the Media Bin, can then be added to the Camtasia Timeline.

You'll work with both options—recording using the PowerPoint recorder add-in and importing PowerPoint as images—during the next few activities.

> **Note:** The next activity is for PC users only because the Camtasia add-in is not available on the Mac. **Mac users**, you can skip ahead to the activity on page 151.

Guided Activity 52: Record PowerPoint on the PC

1. If Camtasia is running, close the program.

2. Open a PowerPoint presentation with Microsoft PowerPoint.

   ☐ using **Microsoft PowerPoint**, open **S3_Policies** from the **Camtasia2023Data > Other_Assets** folder

   The Camtasia PowerPoint Add-in is automatically installed on your computer by the Camtasia application installer. Unless it has been disabled, you should be greeted with the dialog box below. (You can also confirm that the Camtasia Add-in has been installed by choosing **File > Options > Add-ins** from within PowerPoint.)

   ☐ click the **OK** button

3. Review the Camtasia PowerPoint tools.

   ☐ on the **PowerPoint Ribbon**, click the **Add-Ins** tab

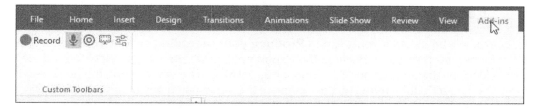

   Camtasia recording tools appear at the left of the Add-ins tab.

4. Record the PowerPoint presentation.

   ☐ from the **Custom Toolbars** area, click the **Record** tool

   The PowerPoint slide show begins.

   ☐ in the lower right screen, click the **Click to begin recording** button

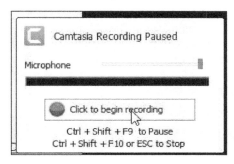

   At this point, the presentation is being recorded, much like your screen was recorded when you learned to use the Camtasia Recorder (on page 22).

   ☐ take your time and click in the middle of each slide to progress through the slide show

   When you reach the end of the slide show, the alert dialog box shown below appears.

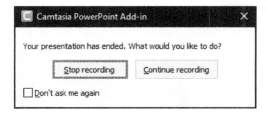

   ☐ click the **Stop Recording** button

You are prompted to save the recording.

❑ navigate to the **Camtasia2023Data** folder

❑ open the **Video_Files** folder and then save the file

You will be asked if you'd like to **Produce your recording** or **Edit your recording**. The former will take you directly to the Export options where you can elect to produce the video for Screencast, for YouTube, or as HTML5. The latter opens the recording in the Camtasia Editor where you can enhance the video using any of the production techniques you've learned to add during the lessons throughout this book (add annotations, audio, quizzes, behaviors, images, videos, etc.).

❑ select **Edit your recording**

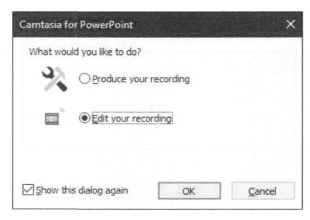

❑ click the **OK** button

The PowerPoint presentation is added to the Camtasia Media Bin. At this point, you could add the video to the Timeline, add annotations, audio, animations, and then export the project as you have learned to do throughout this book.

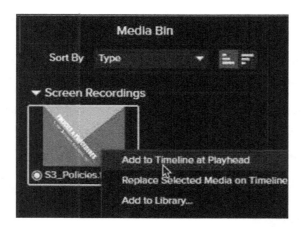

Guided Activity 53: Import a PowerPoint Presentation

1. **All users:** Create a new Camtasia project (there is no need to save previous projects).

2. Import PowerPoint slides into Camtasia as images.

   ☐ choose **File > Import > Media**

   ☐ from **Camtasia2023Data > Other_Assets**, open **S3_Policies**

   PC users, the PowerPoint slides are automatically added to the Media Bin as individual images. **Mac users,** you'll see a dialog box where you can elect to import all of the slides or select from a range of slides (you should import all of the slides).

   ☐ **Mac users**: click the **Import** button

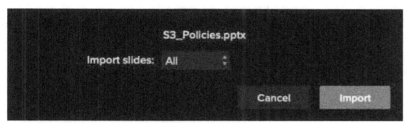

Above, Mac users will see the option to import all of the PowerPoint slides or a range.

At the left, the imported PowerPoint slides appear on the Camtasia Media Bin.

Note: I sometimes receive "memory" error messages when attempting to import a PowerPoint presentation, even though my computer has plenty of memory. If the PowerPoint import process did not work or you received an error message, start PowerPoint prior to attempting to import the slides into Camtasia. Leave PowerPoint running until the import process is finished.

3. Add multiple images to the Timeline at one time.

   ☐ on the **Media Bin**, select any one of the images

   ☐ PC users, press [**ctrl**] [**a**] to select all of the images
   Mac users, press [**command**] [**a**] to select all of the images

   ☐ right-click any of one of the imported images and choose
   Add to Timeline at Playhead

NOTES

Closed Captions

Closed captioning allows you to provide descriptive information in your published eLearning project that typically matches the voiceover audio in your Camtasia project.

There are a few ways that you can add closed captions to a Camtasia project. The following activities show you how to create the captions manually by typing what you hear in the media.

If you have the original voiceover script, you can copy and paste the text into a Camtasia caption, one line at a time.

If you're using Camtasia for the PC, you can use Camtasia's Speech-to-Text feature to have Camtasia transcribe the speech into captions. While this technique sounds ideal, I've had limited success with this feature and find that I need to review the resulting text and make significant corrections.

In my experience, the methods described so far are too labor-intensive. The best and fastest way to add captions to a Camtasia project is via SubRips, otherwise known as SRTs. An SRT is a raw closed caption file format containing the text from an audio file *and* the audio timing. Websites like REV (rev.com) allow you to upload audio files and, for as little as $1 per minute of audio, receive downloadable SRT files. The SRTs are then imported into Camtasia as captions and synchronized with the corresponding audio media on the Timeline.

The process of creating closed captions is a bit different between the PC and Mac, so I've split them up. PC users, your activity appears below. Mac users, you can skip ahead to the "Create Mac Closed Captions" module which begins on page 162.

Guided Activity 54: Manually Create PC Closed Captions

1. Open the **CaptionMe** project. (When prompted to save the project from the last activity, there is no need to do so.)

   There are seven audio files in the **Voiceover** track. You'll need to listen to and then type the audio you hear as closed captions.

2. Open the Captions tool.

   ☐ choose **View > Tools > Captions**

3. Add captions manually.

   ☐ on the **Timeline**, position the **Playhead** at **5;00** (this is where the first voiceover audio clip is positioned)

   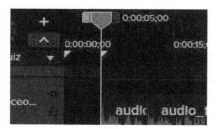

   ☐ on the **Canvas**, click the **Play** button and listen to the audio

   In this first audio segment, the narrator says: "Welcome to Super Simplistic Solutions learning series. This is lesson one: Creating New Folders."

❑ on the **Timeline**, re-position the **Playhead** at exactly **5;00**

❑ on the **Captions** panel, click **Add Caption**

A callout is added to both Track 4 and the Canvas.

❑ on the **Canvas**, type the following into the Caption area:
Welcome to Super Simplistic Solutions learning series.

4. Format the Caption text.

❑ click the **Font Properties** drop-down menu and change the **Size** to **24**

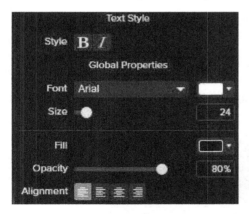

The Americans with Disabilities Act (ADA), a 1990 US civil rights law, prohibits discrimination against individuals with disabilities. Generally speaking, the ADA exists to ensure that people with disabilities have the same rights and opportunities as everyone else. The law guarantees equal opportunity for individuals with disabilities in public accommodations, employment, transportation, state and local government services, website experiences, and even eLearning.

When creating eLearning content, you should avoid doing anything in your project that does not conform to ADA standards. In the image below, the new Caption's font size is not ADA-compliant as indicated by the X to the right of the Font Properties drop-down menu.

5. Make Caption font formatting ADA-compliant.

   ☐ click the **ADA Compliance** drop-down menu

   ☐ click the **Make Compliant** button

The Caption's formatting conforms to ADA standards as indicated by the check mark.

6. Add another Caption.

   ☐ on the **Timeline**, position the Playhead to the right of the first Caption

   ☐ from the **Captions** panel, click the **Add Caption** button

   ☐ in the Caption area on the Canvas, type **This is lesson one: Creating New Folders.**

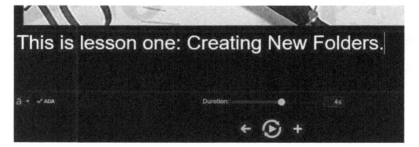

Guided Activity 55: Control PC Caption Timing

1. Ensure that the **CaptionMe** project is open.

2. Zoom closer to the Timeline.

3. On the **Timeline**, notice that the first Callout is onscreen about a second and a half too long. The vertical line in the image below indicates when the narrator has finished saying the word "series."

It's a best practice to synchronize the audio and the timing of the Captions. In this instance, you need to shorten the Caption's playtime.

4. Adjust Caption Timing

☐ on the **Timeline**, drag the **right** edge of the **first** Caption to the **left** a bit to shorten its play time

PC Captions Confidence Check

1. Move the second Caption left so it lines up with the audio as shown below.

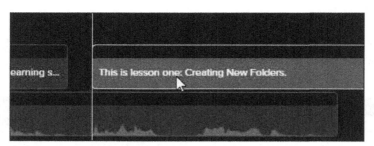

2. Shorten the playtime of the second Caption so it matches the audio.

3. Add a third caption just to the right of the first two containing this text: **This lesson is going to teach you how to create a new folder on your computer.**

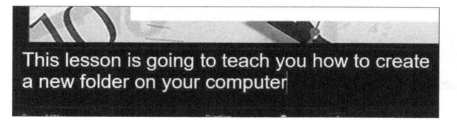

4. If necessary, make adjustments to the Caption's timing so it matches the audio as closely as possible.

5. Export the project as a **Legacy Local File** > **Custom Production Settings**.

6. On the **Smart Player Options**, select the **Options** tab.

   From this screen, you can enable or disable Captions and make their default state "visible" or "on by default." The standard is to make Captions not visible by default, so leaving **Captions initially visible** deselected is fine as-is.

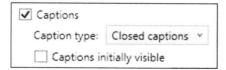

7. Click the remaining **Next** buttons and as you move through the screens, disable both the SCORM and Watermark options.

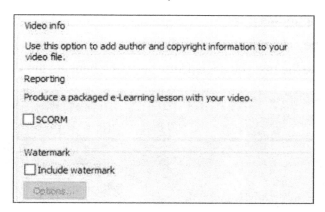

8. Click the **Finish** button to finish the export process. (Export the files to the **Produced_Videos** folder.)

9. View the video in your web browser.

10. On the Player, click the **CC** button to view the Captions.

11. Close the browser window.

12. Back in Camtasia, close the Production Results window.

As you have learned, you can type the closed caption text manually. However, if you have access to a voiceover script, you can reuse that content to create the captions.

13. Minimize Camtasia and, from the **Camtasia2023Data**, **Other_Assets** folder, open **CreatingFoldersVoiceoverScript** using Microsoft Word.

Audio File 1:
Welcome to Super Simplistic Solutions learning series.
This is lesson one: Creating New Folders.

Audio File 2:
This lesson is going to teach you how to create a new folder on your computer, how to rename it, and how to both delete and restore recycled items.

Audio File 3:
When creating folders keep in mind that you can create as many folders as you need.

14. In the **Audio File 2** text section, select **"how to rename it, and how to both delete and restore recycled items"** and copy the text to the Clipboard.

15. Return to Camtasia and the **CaptionMe** project.

16. Position the Playhead just to the right of your existing Captions.

17. Create a new Caption and paste the text you copied into the space beneath the Canvas.

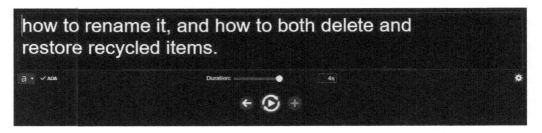

18. Save your work.

Guided Activity 56: Use Speech-to-Text to Create Captions

1. Ensure that the **CaptionMe** project is open.

2. Remove a track and its media.

   ☐ on the **Timeline**, right-click **Track 4** and choose **Remove Track**

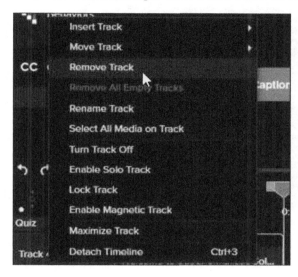

   Because there is media on the track, you are prompted to confirm the action.

   ☐ click the **Yes** button

3. Create Captions using Speech-to-Text.

   ☐ from the upper left of the **Captions** panel, click **Script Options** (the **gear** icon)

   ☐ choose **Speech-to-Text**

   You'll receive some tips for improving the Speech-to-Text feature. Later, after you've had a chance to work with Camtasia, you should try some of these tips and see how they

improve the Speech-to-Text results. For this activity, you're going to use the default settings and see where they take you.

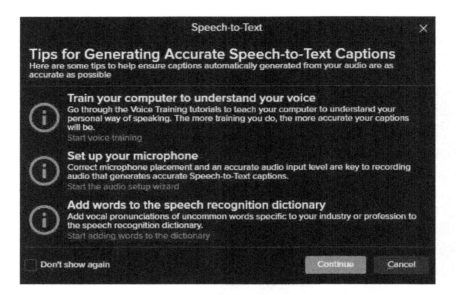

☐ click the **Continue** button

Camtasia "listens" to the voiceover audio in the background and, like magic, creates Captions on a new Track 4.

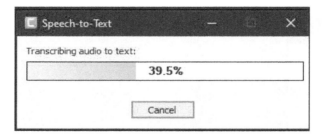

Look through the Timeline and notice in the image below that although much of the audio was transcribed nicely, many of the Captions need editing.

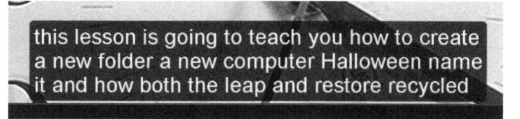

this lesson is going to teach you how to create a new folder a new computer Halloween name it and how both the leap and restore recycled

You've now learned three ways to create Captions: transcribing, copy/paste from a script, and Speech-to-Text. Now let's see how well SRTs work.

Guided Activity 57: Import Captions on the PC

1. Ensure that the **CaptionMe** project is open.

2. Remove a track and its media.

   ❑ on the **Timeline**, right-click **Track 4** and choose **Remove Track**

   Because there is once again media on the track, you are prompted to confirm the action.

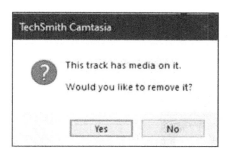

   ❑ click the **Yes** button

3. Import a caption.

   ❑ choose **File > Import > Captions**
   ❑ from **Camtasia2023Data > Audio_Files > SRT Files**, open **audio_file01.srt**

   The caption is added to Track 4. Because the SRT file contains the voiceover script text *and* the timing, the playtime of the caption is an exact match for the audio_file01 media in the voiceover track.

4. Reposition a caption on the Timeline.

   ❑ on the **Timeline**, drag the caption in Track 4 until its **left edge** aligns with the **audio_file01** media in the Voiceover track

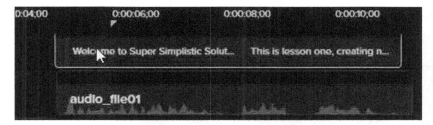

5. Save your work.

   The next few activities on Captions are for Mac users. PC users, you can skip ahead to page 171 and learn about Templates.

Guided Activity 58: Create Mac Closed Captions

1. Save and close any open projects.

2. Open the **CaptionMe** project.

   There are several audio clips in the Voiceover track. You're going to listen to some of the clips and create a few captions.

3. Add captions manually.

   ☐ from the tools at the left, click **Audio Effects**

   ☐ from the list of Audio Effects, drag **Captions** on top of the first audio clip in the Voiceover Track (on the **Timeline**)

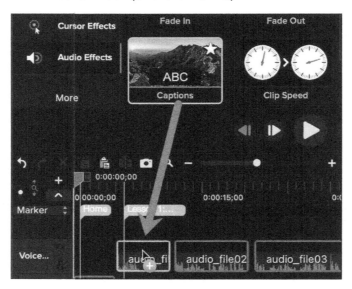

The Caption track opens just above the Timeline.

   ☐ on the **Caption track**, click the **left side** of the audio waveform

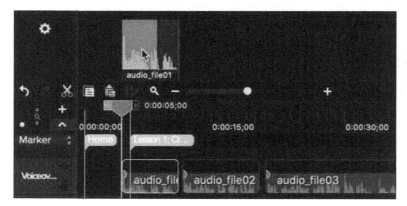

The first part of the audio plays and a typing area opens. In this first audio segment, the narrator says: **Welcome to Super Simplistic Solutions learning series. This is lesson one: Creating New Folders.**

❑ type the following into the space beneath the background image: **Welcome to Super Simplistic Solutions learning series.**

The caption you typed automatically appears on the Canvas. This is what learners will see if they view the lesson's closed captions.

4. Format the Caption text.

❑ on the **Caption track**, double-click the left side of the audio file

❑ on the caption, click the **Change font properties for captions** tool

The Font options open.

NOTES

☐ change the font size to **18**

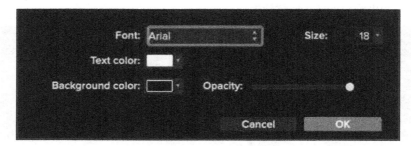

☐ click the **OK** button

On the Canvas, the change to the font size is immediate. Although the smaller font size might look better than the larger font, keep in mind that the closed captions aren't necessarily for you—they're typically meant to help learners who cannot hear the audio. When creating eLearning content, you'll need to be on the alert to anything you might do in your project that does not conform to the Americans with Disabilities Act (ADA).

In case you're not familiar with the ADA, it's a 1990 US civil rights law that prohibits discrimination against individuals with disabilities in all areas of public life, including jobs, schools, transportation, and all public and private places that are open to the general public. Generally speaking, the law exists to ensure that people with disabilities have the same rights and opportunities as everyone else and guarantees equal opportunity for individuals with disabilities in public accommodations, employment, transportation, state and local government services, and even eLearning.

In the case of font sizes used in captions, a larger font is preferred because it is easier to see and read on a computer screen or mobile device.

5. Restore the Caption's font size to its larger size.

    ☐ on the **Caption track**, click the left side of the audio file again

    ☐ click the **Change font properties for captions** tool

    ☐ change the font size back to **32**

    ☐ click the **OK** button

6. Add another Caption.

    ☐ on the **Caption track**, click the **right** side of the audio waveform

    ☐ type **This is lesson one: Creating New Folders.**

7. Preview the project from the beginning of the Timeline.

   The captions appear, but they do not exactly match the voiceover audio. For instance, the first caption is onscreen a bit too long. You'll fix that next.

Guided Activity 59: Control Mac Caption Timing

1. Ensure that the **CaptionMe.cmproj** project is open.

2. Adjust Caption Timing.

    ☐ on the **Caption track**, click the **left side** of the audio file

    ☐ on the Caption panel, change the **Duration** to **3** seconds

3. Preview the project from the beginning of the Timeline.

    The Caption timing is more in sync with the voiceover audio.

Mac Captions Confidence Check

1. Add a caption to the second audio file on the **Timeline** with the following text: **This lesson is going to teach you how to create a new folder on your computer.**

2. Export the project to Screencast. (Prior to clicking the Export button, choose **Closed captions** from the **Caption style** drop-down menu.)

3. After the Export process is complete, Visit the page on Screencast.

4. After starting the lesson, click the **CC** button on the playbar to view the Captions you added.

5. Close the browser window.

   Now you'll get a chance to copy and paste text from an existing voiceover script.

6. Hide Camtasia (to get it out of your way for a moment) and, from the Camtasia2023Data > **Other_Assets** folder, open **CreatingFoldersVoiceoverScript** with Microsoft Word.

> ## Audio File 1:
> Welcome to Super Simplistic Solutions learning series.
> This is lesson one: Creating New Folders.
>
> ## Audio File 2:
> This lesson is going to teach you how to create a new folder on your computer, how to rename it, and how to both delete and restore recycled items.
>
> ## Audio File 3:
> When creating folders keep in mind that you can create as many folders as you need.

NOTES

7. In the **Audio File 2** text, select **"how to rename it, and how to both delete and restore recycled items"** and copy the text to the Clipboard.

8. Return to Camtasia and the CaptionMe project.

9. Still working in the second caption, click the right side of the waveform and paste the text you copied into the caption text area.

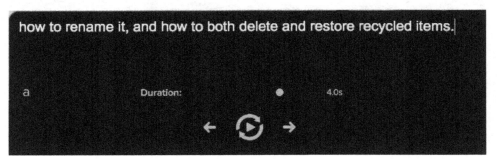

10. Save your work.

Guided Activity 60: Import Captions on the Mac

1. Ensure that the **CaptionMe** project is open.

2. Remove captions.

   ☐ on the **Timeline, Captions panel,** click the **Show caption options** icon 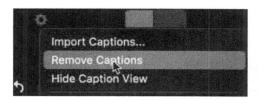 and choose **Remove Captions**

   ☐ click the **OK** button to confirm the action

3. Hide the Captions view.

   ☐ on the **Timeline,** Captions panel, click the **Show caption options** icon ⚙ and choose **Hide Caption View**

4. Import a caption.

   ☐ choose **File > Import > Captions**

   ☐ from **Camtasia2023Data > Audio_Files > SRT Files,** open **audio_file01.srt**

   The caption is added to Track 4. Because the caption file contains the voiceover script text *and* the timing, the playtime of the caption is an exact match for the audio_file01 media in the voiceover track. The caption just needs to be moved on the Timeline to ensure it appears when the audio begins to play.

5. Reposition a caption on the Timeline.

   ☐ on the **Timeline,** drag the caption in Track 4 **right** until its left edge aligns with the **audio_file01** media in the Voiceover track

NOTES

6. Import another caption.

   ❏ choose **File > Import > Captions**

   ❏ from **Camtasia2023Data > Audio_Files > SRT Files**, open **audio_file02.srt**

The caption is added to Track 5.

7. Reposition the caption on the Timeline.

   ❏ on the **Timeline**, drag the caption in Track 5 **right** until its left edge aligns with the **audio_file02** media in the Voiceover track

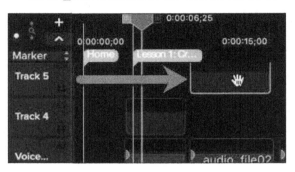

8. Preview the project from the beginning to see the captions on the Canvas.

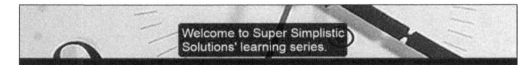

9. Save your work.

10. Close the project.

Templates

Every time you create a new Camtasia project, you're literally starting with a blank canvas. As you've learned during this book, it's easy to fill the Canvas with Library elements, images, annotations, videos, media, and add transitions to media. However, if there are assets and effects that you frequently use in your projects, it's not necessary to start from scratch every time. Instead, you should create a template that contains commonly-used elements. When you create a Camtasia project that uses the template, all of the template's Timeline elements, behaviors, etc., will be retained, saving you all kinds of time as opposed to starting from scratch.

Guided Activity 61: Create and Use a Template

1. Using Camtasia, create a new project.

2. Add a Library asset to the Timeline.

    ❑ from the tools at the left, click **Library**

    ❑ from the **Camtasia 2023** Library assets, open the **Titles** folder

    ❑ right-click **Big Type 1** and choose **Add to Timeline at Playhead**

3. Add a placeholder.

    ❑ position the Playhead at the 20-second mark on the Timeline

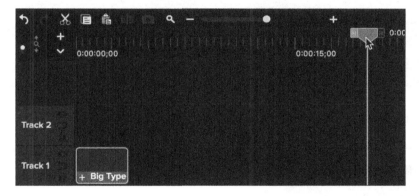

    ❑ choose **Edit > Add Placeholder to Timeline**

    A placeholder is an object that can be replaced with any piece of media from the Media Bin, Library, or Annotations. In this instance, the intent is for anyone using your template to replace the placeholder with a screen recording. You'll add instructions next so that anyone using your template knows what to do with the placeholder.

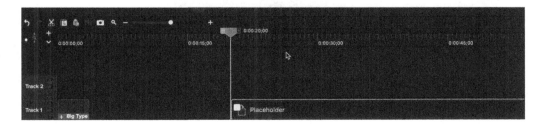

4. Edit Placeholder Properties.

☐ with the Placeholder selected, click in the **Title** area of the Placeholder Properties

☐ type **Screen Recording**

☐ click in the **Notes** field and type **Replace this Placeholder with a screen recording by dragging a video from the Media Bin here.**

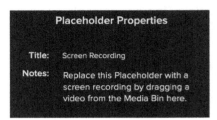

Notice that there's currently a gap between the two Timeline objects, shown highlighted in the image below.

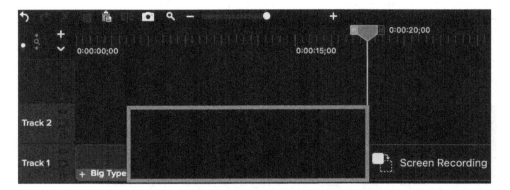

5. Enable Magnetic Tracks.

☐ at the left of **Track 1** on the **Timeline**, click **Enable magnetic track**

The gap between the Timeline objects is removed.

6. Save a project as a template.

☐ choose **File > Save project as template**

The New Template dialog box opens.

☐ name the New Template **Recording Template**

☐ click the **OK** button

PC users, You'll be alerted about how to use the template to create a new project. You can acknowledge the alert dialog box by clicking the **OK** button. **Mac users,** close the Untitled project without saving.

7. Create a project based on the new template.

☐ choose **File > New Project from Template**

The Template Manager opens.

NOTES

☐ select the **Recording Template** you just created

☐ click the **New from Template** button

PC users, you'll be prompted to save the project you used to build the template. You can click the **No** button.

A new project is created that has the elements from your template. At this point, you could replace the placeholder text and object with content of your own, just as you have learned to do during lessons throughout this book.

8. Exit/Quit Camtasia. (There is no need to save any open files if prompted.)

That's a Wrap!

I'd like to congratulate you on completing this book. I'm hoping you are now comfortable with the following Camtasia features:

- ❑ Creating projects and project templates
- ❑ Recording screen actions
- ❑ Adding videos media
- ❑ Adding annotations
- ❑ Adding images
- ❑ Adding behaviors
- ❑ Creating custom animations
- ❑ Controlling the cursor and the cursor path
- ❑ Importing audio
- ❑ Adding closed captions
- ❑ Recording voiceover audio
- ❑ Working on the Timeline
- ❑ Adding quizzes
- ❑ Reporting quiz results to a Learning Management System
- ❑ Importing PowerPoint content into a Camtasia project
- ❑ Exporting content as a video
- ❑ Exporting content as HTML5

If you need help using Camtasia, the first places to look are online via the TechSmith Camtasia website (http://techsmith.com) and the TechSmith blog (blogs.techsmith.com). TechSmith has an awesome community offering free tips, tricks, and step-by-step videos covering all things Camtasia. You can also email me at **ksiegel@iconlogic.com** if you need a nudge in the right direction. Lastly, I offer live, virtual Camtasia mentoring and development services and onsite or virtual group training.

NOTES

Notes

Index

NOTES

NOTES

Notes

Made in the USA
Monee, IL
18 August 2023

41198415R10111